Ministry of Sound:

The Manual

by Bill Brewster
and Frank Broughton

001

HEADLINE

Written by Frank Broughton
and Bill Brewster

Copyright © Ministry of Sound 1998

The right of the Ministry of Sound to
be identified as the Author of the Work
has been asserted by them in
accordance with the Copyright,
Designs and Patents Act 1988.

First published in 1998 by
Headline Book Publishing

10 9 8 7 6 5 4 3 2 1

ISBN 0 7472 7636 6

Printed and bound in Italy by
Canale & C. Sp. A.

Headline Book Publishing
a division of Hodder Headline PLC
338 Euston Road
London NW1 3BH

"You don't think I look like Leo Sayer do you?" Keith, The Prodigy

Contents

005

The DJs

The Music

"I want to send a message to the Spice Girls. Tell them I'll deal with them one at a time or all at once. It doesn't matter to me." Snoop Doggy Dogg

ju

007

"Britain is a really good market for bad drugs." Dutch drugs tester in Mixmag

The History of DJing and the Origins of House

The Godfather of the modern DJ is a little known Brooklyn-born man called Francis Grasso. Although DJs had emerged in the immediate post-war period, with prototype discotheques first opening in Paris, New York and London in the sixties, it was at a club called the Sanctuary that Grasso laid down the blueprint for what was to follow. Previously, DJs had either talked between the records or had simply laid down one record after another, usually mixing current pop and rock hits rather than playing records specifically crafted for the dancefloor.

Grasso became a DJ by accident, after the regular DJ at Salvation II, the club Grasso worked at, failed to show. He immediately discovered an aptitude for it. By the late-sixties, he had become resident at the Sanctuary, an uninhibited gay club on 43rd Street and 10th Avenue (ironically, Grasso was probably the only straight person in the club). Unlike many DJs of the period, Grasso eschewed the staple of Hot 100 tunes for a mixture of R&B based records (Gladys Knight & The Pips, Booker T & The MGs, Aretha Franklin), freaky rock tracks like Chicago's 'I'm A Man' and African chant records by the likes of Olatunji (the producer of the original version of Candido's Salsoul classic 'Jingo').

He was the first person to blend records into one another, at the same time inventing the technique of 'slip-cueing' — holding the record he was cueing-up stationary while the turntable beneath it spun. In this way the record would start immediately when it was released, making it easier to get the beats from the two records to match up.

His style became yet more inventive when he acquired a Thorens turntable with pitch control (the forerunner of today's Technics 1200), enabling him to blend records for minutes at a time.

Taking, for example, the drum break from 'I'm A Man', he would lay the wails from Led Zeppelin's 'Whole Lotta Love' over the top to create a trippy fusion of sounds, pre-empting the custom-made disco mixes that emerged in the mid-seventies.

If Francis Grasso is the unsung pioneer of DJing, then David Mancuso of the Loft is its inspiration. Interview any of the current older crop of New York DJs and Mancuso's name usually figures. He was the man who inspired legends like Walter Gibbons, Shep Pettibone and Larry Levan to DJ. Though less technically adept than Grasso, Mancuso utilised his encyclopaedic knowledge of music to devastating effect on the dancefloor, whipping the dancers into undulating sexual peaks and troughs of musical ecstasy. Though his music selection is what he's perhaps best known

for, his greatest contribution was probably the sound system — custom-built — that he constructed in the club. No-one had ever heard anything like it. Levan recalled: "David called up manufacturers Cerwin-Vega and they made these 1000 watt bass drivers. They sounded incredible."

If the techniques were there, and the sound systems had the power to drive the music, what was needed next was better quality vinyl — at this point, DJs played straight from 7" and LP. How the 12" was created is open to conjecture. One story has it that disco-DJ Tom Moulton — who did work for underground dance label Salsoul — had been to a cutting plant to get a mix put on to vinyl and all they had was 12" vinyl so he told them to use that instead. At a club called Galaxy 21 later that night, Moulton handed the disc to the resident DJ, Walter Gibbons, who immediately noticed the extra power and resolution using less crammed grooves. Another story is that an employee at RCA, David Todd, created the first 12" as a promotion to DJs. The record was Vickie Sue Robinson's 'Never Gonna Let You Go' and was never made commerically available. Whichever story is true, the first commercially available 12" was certainly Double Exposure's 'Ten Percent' on Salsoul. This was also remarkable for its content. Originally a three-minute LP track, Walter Gibbons transformed it into an eleven-minute monster of dubbed-out disco and drums. Until then, Salsoul and other disco labels had featured heavily orchestrated songs (based on the original Philly sound pioneered at Sigma studios), but Gibbons began the trend for tracks to be stripped down to the barest essential of rhythm, voice and song, a trend that reached its logical conclusion with house ten years later.

Radical change for both production and DJing was also signalled by the introduction of computer technology into dance music. Previously, producing a dance record required a decent studio, adept musicians, vocalists and string sections. Computers dispensed with this need. Although they had been used in records as early as Timmy Thomas's 'Why Can't We Live Together' in 1972, the technology was not of sufficiently high quality until the early to mid-eighties when early samplers such as the Fairlight (as pioneered by Peter Gabriel) and drum machines such as the Linn and Roland's TR-808 and 909 series became available. It should be noted that some of the early samplers were so large, they virtually filled whole rooms.

Almost imperceptibly, dance music began to evolve with New York productions such as D-Train's 'You're The One For Me' and Peech Boys' 'Don't Make Me Wait' incorporating much of the new electronic technology, while still reproducing the classic soul sound that had been American black music's hallmark. Meanwhile, across in Chicago…

No-one is certain how the term 'house' came about (though the smart money says it's an abbreviation of 'Warehouse', the name of the club where Frankie Knuckles was resident from the early-eighties). All we do know is that it changed the face of

dance music forever. Essentially it was a stripped down continuation of disco. As Farley Jackmaster Funk relates: "What came up with house music was that I took a TR-808 drum machine and put a four/four in and played the old Philly sound on it." Whether Farley was the first is open to debate (not known as an innovator, the idea for his big hit, 'Love Can't Turn Around', a cover of an Isaac Hayes song, was 'borrowed' from his then room-mate Steve 'Silk' Hurley).

While all these technological and technical innovations were happening in the States, the UK was still lagging behind. In the Britain of the late-seventies, even mixing was a still a relatively rare phenomenon. The real innovator of UK mixing was an unknown by the name of Greg James. James was a Philadelphia-based jock, not especially well known in the US, who was brought over to this country by Steven Hayter, the promoter at the Embassy, in London in 1978. Producer Ian Levine recalls his arrival: "Steven's idea was to give that classic gay New York disco thing to the English. They were trying to do a Studio 54 with the Embassy. In 1978 it became huge. London had never seen anything like it. It was the first club ever in England to have a proper lighting system and a sound system and mixing records. Nobody had ever mixed before." Later on, it was James who would also teach seminal

British soul/dance DJs, Les Adams and Froggy to mix. James also ran a store called Spin-Offs, where a young man called Jazzy M worked.

However, 'personality' jocks still held sway, although there were plenty of other DJs who programmed the records without the talking (Ian Dewhirst at the Warehouse in Leeds; Ian Levine at Heaven; Graeme Park at the Garage in Nottingham; The Haçienda DJs; the Soul Mafia and others in London). What inevitably changed this was the arrival of house to Britain, with jocks like Mark Moore, Colin Faver and the Watson brothers, Morris and Noel. The simple fact was that house made mixing physically much easier since the beats were computer programmed and so, unlike a live drummer, never veered out of time. DJs also discovered that each tune didn't necessarily have to stand up on their own, that they could build up to climactic peaks by programming and mixing the records together. The epoch of the DJ-as-artist was born. Things would never be the same again.

Sound
Systems

012

Not only is New York the home of hip hop, electro, the modern DJ and unfeasibly large sandwiches, it is also the cradle of club sound systems.

The great clubs in the city — the Loft, Paradise Garage, Sound Factory — were all built around two key elements: the sound systems and the DJ. Compare and contrast that to the majority of club owners in the UK for whom the sound system is often just below the barman's uniform in a list of priorities.

How many times have you been to a club where it appears they are piping the music through a large bowl of custard? David Mancuso was the first person to put the sound system first for his parties at the Loft in New York. Amongst the goodies installed were Klipsch-horns (designed in the twenties by Paul Klipsch), Mark Levinson amplifiers, and Koetsu hand-crafted cartridges. Top manufacturer Cerwin-Vega even built a 1000 watt bass driver to his specifications, which Larry Levan enthused: "They sounded incredible. He would do things like play the sound system with the bass and tweeters off and as whatever record was peaking — bang! — they would all come on."

Levan's own Paradise Garage was heavily influenced by what he had experienced at the Loft (Levan was revered as a fine sound engineer who could draw crisp sounds out of the murkiest system). Along with Richard Long, he designed a system which became the blueprint and inspiration for many other clubs worldwide. Justin Berkman, one of the founders of the Ministry of Sound recalls going to the Garage for the first time: "From the first Saturday night I went in there, I pretty much wanted to be a DJ; and the main focus was to play at the Garage on that system." When the Ministry eventually opened, the system was supplied by Long's associates (Long himself died in the mid-eighties).

A little taste of New York has been imported to the UK via sound engineers, Steve Dash and George Smith. It was they who furnished the Sound Factory, Twilo and Sound Factory Bar with thousands of watts of pure power; and it was they who supplied the £750,000 system at Cream in Liverpool. The specifications for each room are now drawn up on computer, giving a more accurate idea of sound distribution. Away from the technical talk, a good system — apart from enhancing the sound of the records played — is less harmful to the naked ear. As Steve Dash says, "You want the sound to be intense and clean but you don't want the mid-range horns to part your ears."

A club's volume is such that there are already a few putative Pete Townshends in the DJ world. There is now a Harley Street specialist doing a roaring trade in couture ear-plugs at £150 a throw. Not to mention clubbers themselves. By law, any worker exposed to more than eight hours of noise at level of 90 decibels (dB(A)) has to wear protection. Imagine then, the damage you may be doing to your ears if the average club runs at a level of around 120-125 dB(A). Think of those poor souls asleep in the bassbin next time you go out. Tinnitus — that horrible ringing in the ears — is rife amongst nightfolk (it's estimated that 80% of clubbers experience it on first leaving the club). Dr Jonathan Hazell of the Royal National Institute of the Deaf believes that, "each time you go clubbing you trigger tinnitus and increase the risk it may become permanent at some point." How many of you still have ringing in your ears come Monday morning? We are potentially breeding a culture in which our generation will be half deaf by the time they reach forty-five.

But Mark Anderson of the British Tinnitus Association has some simple advice for clubbers: "Put a good space between you and the speakers. Give your ears a rest. Go to the toilet, have a drink somewhere quiet. Research shows that even ten minutes in an hour can make a serious difference." You have been warned.

"There are millions of people in Detroit and I'd say about thirty of them have heard of techno." Marc Kinchen, 1990

Bands

A TASTE OF ORIENTAL SPLENDOUR

MINISTRY OF SOUND, LONDON

**Live performances by Slacker
and Beat Foundation**

DJ's Dave Seaman, Paul Van Dyke,
Andry Nalin (Nalin & Kane), Ian Ossia,
Nigel Dawson, Anthony Pappa,
Daniele Davoli, Quivvey, Danny Hussian,
DJ Pippi (Pacha) and Jazzy M.

Special guests Nuphonic Records with
Dave Hill, Jools Butterfield and
Simon Lee (Faze Action).

SATURDAY 14TH MARCH 1998

9pm-9am. Advance tickets £30.00.

For further information please contact
Renaissance on 01782 717872/3.
Ministry Of Sound on 0171 378 6528.
Ministry Of Sound, 103 Gaunt Street, London.

TICKETS

6TH BIRTHDAY PARTY

"If You Want To Get Down, Get Down On Your Knees." Displayed on banner by
religious protesters at opening of Limelight, NYC, which occupied a disused church.

It doesn't take a DJ to make you move. The first music was undoubtedly for dancing; so too jazz, rock 'n' roll and rhythm and blues. Motown was dance music, everyone knows of James Brown and George Clinton's contributions and even rock acts often managed to slip an uptempo number on their albums. Bands have always been central to dance: here are six which made more of a difference than most. Respect also to The Shamen, Primal Scream, Stone Roses, Underworld, Leftfield, Orbital, Massive Attack, Stereo MCs, New Order…

Kraftwerk

Talking Heads

Happy Mondays

Kraftwerk were making techno back when Detroit still made cars. They were hardly a laugh a minute — four Germans dressed as robot librarians certainly didn't look like they had a dancefloor explosion hidden in their party-pants — but they were probably more influential to modern dance music than any other single group. Most British ears heard sterilised Europop. America reacted to the Düsseldorf quartet's minimalist music as if it were morse code from Mars. Upon hearing 1977's 'Trans-Europe Express', Afrika Bambaataa went home and invented electro and then hip hop, Levan and Kevorkian perfected the dance dub, Chicago came up with house, and, in Detroit, a whole Kraftwerkist religion was founded, its holy father Derrick May joking that techno was "just George Clinton and Kraftwerk stuck in an elevator together." Still together, Kraftwerk made a triumphal return to the dance community they helped inspire at Tribal Gathering 97.

Apart from being the kind of ultrahip Manhattan musos who frequented the happening underground clubs of the we-don't-care eighties, Talking Heads were also the kind of ultrahip Manhattan musos whose records were actually played there. David Byrne's group was the spearhead of a bunch of skinny new-wavers who were doing in music what the great DJs were busy doing with records: combining the nerdy art-school pose of soulless synthpop with the dirt-digging rhythms of soul, funk and reggae to emerge with the meaning of dance. Other white funkers like Was Not Was, The Police and even the Rolling Stones, figured too, but it was Talking Heads, along with their breakaway rhythm section Tom Tom Club, who stood out from the pack for their willingness to plunder African and Afro-Cuban rhythms, their insistent basslines and their sheer danceability.

Five men who looked like they'd just ripped off your car battery loping around a stage making the most slackish smoked-out dub-done-disco, while a sixth member — a maraca-waving marionette with eyeballs like eight-balls — stared into the crowd and exhorted them to dance. In a reverse of the normal rock 'n' roll ethos, Shaun Ryder insisted that the Happy Mondays were a musical habit formed around some serious drug-taking. They were always meant to be a dance group (Mike Pickering produced their first single and Paul Oakenfold produced their most famous songs), and around 1989 when the world had caught up with their pharmaceuticals they dissolved the band/audience division to make a concert hall just as appropriate a place to dance and take drugs as a club or a rave. Along the way, with bands like James, Inspiral Carpets, Stone Roses, 808 State, they defined a city — Madchester — and a style — floppy-fashioned neo-psychedelia — which made London feel dull and provincial for a long while.

Essential tracks
'Numbers'
'Trans-Europe Express'

Essential tracks
Talking Heads: 'Once In a Lifetime'
Tom-Tom Club: 'Genius Of Love',
'Wordy Rappinghood'

Essential tracks
'Step On'
'Loose Fit'

M People

Driving piano anthems painted a dark red shade of non-drip gloss, the composition completed by the spine-shivering depth of Heather Small's unmistakable voice — "What people like most about M People," says their main songwriter Paul Heard sagely, "seems to be the music." House was always too good to be confined in a box marked 'underground', and M People are the proof that what works in a club can also have the nation's mums and dads humming along to the radio over breakfast. The M stands for Mike, as in Pickering, one of those people whose career neatly shadowed the development of dance, and most famously the DJ helmsman of Manchester's Haçienda for a nine-year stint between 1984 and 1993. Pickering conceived of the band as a front for his production, but quickly realised that what he'd created was a living, breathing monster all set to hammer home the fact that house was now the new pop. Touring with a live band emphasised the point and albums like 'Northern Soul', 'Bizarre Fruit' and 'Elegant Slumming', were so universal in their musicality that they were equally at home on Radio 2 as they were on a busy dancefloor.

Essential Tracks
'Moving On Up'
'One Night In Heaven'

The Prodigy

"Rave is dead and The Prodigy killed it," proclaimed Mixmag in 1992, putting Liam on its cover with a gun to his head as the Essex boy wonders counted the cash from their two cartoon crossover rave choons, 'Charly' and 'Everybody In The Place'. Liam obviously never pulled the trigger because the Prodigy went from there — being rave's novelty pop stars — to the heights of being a killer live band that actually broke America. Remembering that before it meant techno hoover noises, 'hardcore' once meant fast punk guitars, they took the excitement of a rave and turned it into a live music spectacle, then they got even more exciting, until they realised they had turned into punk rockers after all. Though they were named after a keyboard — a Moog Prodigy — they are one of the few rave-borne groups to escape the 'boffins-with-black-boxes' trap and, by taking dance music the furthest it could get from the black gay origins of house, they've made it acceptable to rock-loving white America, even if Keith does look just like a pierced Ronald McDonald.

Essential Tracks
'Everybody In The Place'
'Firestarter'

The Chemical Brothers

Ed Simons and Tom Rowlands, brothers in dust, took all the disaffected house-haters and turned them onto dance music by a different route, their block-rocking beats pushing back the limits of musical magpie-ism. Their sets threw together all of music's fringes from re-heated electro, via obscure dub techno to the rock world's leftovers, an approach forged at The Sunday Social, the London club they started in 1994, where dissected loops of disco linked arms with full-on acid and Beatles records. Sneaking up on the audience created by the lad-friendly techno of bands like Leftfield and Underworld, they remixed their way to full band status, threw out seminal LPs like 'Exit Planet Dust' and 'Dig Your Own Hole', and proved that four-on-the-floor rhythms weren't the only way to shake a crowd's hips.

Essential Tracks
'Chemical Beats'
'Block-Rocking Beats'

20
Dance Records
That Shook
The World

This is in no way meant to be a definitive list. Neither is it meant to be the best records ever made. It is, however, a modest list of records that we believe shaped the way that dance music is today.

Some of these records are nearly thirty years old; some were made in the nineties. Some don't sound so great today; some are still fantastic and still get played.

If you owned these twenty, you would know how dance music came to sound like it does today.

Enjoy.

The Quintessential JB Record
James Brown
'Funky Drummer'
(Polydor 1970)

The First Disco Record
MFSB
'Love Is The Message'
(Philadelphia International 1973)

A Defining Jazz-Funk Record
Lonnie Liston Smith
'Expansions '
(RCA 1975)

The First Commercially Available Twelve-Inch Record
Double Exposure
'Ten Percent'
(Salsoul 1976)

The Greatest Euro-Disco Record
Donna Summer
'I Feel Love'
(Casablanca 1977)

The Minister of the New Super Heavy Funk, now nearing his 70th birthday, remains one the most influential figures in black music, acting as inspiration for everyone from Prince to Parliament. Journalist Nelson George once said James Brown's records were, "as tense and sparse as a Hemmingway short story, though admittedly a lot easier to dance to." This 1970 cut, featuring the mesmerising polyrhythms of JB's drummer Clyde Stubblefield, enjoyed a revival in the eighties thanks to the rare groove warehouse scene (which gave rise to Soul II Soul, Brand New Heavies etc). It has also provided the basis for countless hip hop cuts as well as barrel-loads of cheese such as Candy Flip's version of 'Strawberry Fields Forever'.

Probably the first widely recognised disco record. Although over eleven minutes in length, the first half is, frankly, a bit of a damp squib; the real disco action kicks off in the latter part with a Rhodes and sax-led funkathon. MFSB members, bassist Ronnie Baker, drummer Earl Young and guitarist Norman Harris became the backbone of many other classic outfits on Philly International and, later, Salsoul, including Double Exposure, First Choice, Trammps and the Salsoul Orchestra.

If one record epitomises the late-seventies/early-eighties jazz-funk scene, it's 'Expansions'. Smith, who played keyboards for Art Blakey and Miles Davis amongst many, recorded it in 1975 and it became an instant hit, thanks to its fusion of spacey keyboards, flute solos and Latin-esque rhythms. It has been re-released several times since. Stetsasonic later stole the bassline for their hip hop classic 'Talking All That Jazz'.

Important for two reasons. Firstly, it was one of the first records that Walter Gibbons, influential DJ and remixer in the seventies, worked on, transforming it from its original three minutes to a ten minute stripped-bare epic of modern disco. Secondly, it was the first commercially available twelve-inch single. And that's reason enough for it to be included here.

Born Ladonna Gaines in 1948 in Boston, Mass., Summer found fame in Germany through Italian producer Giorgio Moroder and his Munich-based Oasis label. Although 'Love To Love You Baby' was the track that gave her the first hit, 'I Feel Love' and, in particular Patrick Cowley's 1982 remix of it — all fifteen minutes of sequenced electronic futurism with Summer's breathy vocals atop — remains the definitive Eurodisco track and is still a dancefloor staple.

An Influential Rhythm Record
Chic
'Good Times'
(Atlantic 1979)

An Early Garage Record
D-Train
'You're The One For Me'
(Prelude/Epic 1981)

The First Electro Record
Afrika Bambaataa & The Soul Sonic Force
'Planet Rock'
(Tommy Boy 1981)

The First Ecstasy Record
Soft Cell
'Memorabilia'
(Some Bizarre LP track 1981)

The First No. 1 House Record
Steve 'Silk' Hurley
'Jack Your Body'
(DJ International/London 1987)

Sampled by Sugarhill Gang for the first hip hop hit 'Rapper's Delight', sort of nicked for Queen's 'Another One Bites The Dust', and utilised ever since by loads of R&B acts, very few records have had as much influence on dance music as 'Good Times' and few producers as much as Chic's Bernard Edwards and Nile Rogers. From underground clubs to weddings, it's a record that still gets played today and still sounds great whatever the context. A hugely influential rhythm and a proper classic.

This project (along with Peech Boy's 'Don't Make Me Wait'), fronted by James Williams and mixed by dance innovator François Kevorkian, prefigured the garage sound of the late-eighties by several years. Utilising electronic rhythms and keyboards, Kevorkian created a futuristic soul sound which also incorporated elements of dub reggae. Uplifting.

Produced by John Robie and the legendary Arthur Baker (of Rocker's Revenge, Freeez and the Criminal Element Orchestra), this early example of electro was based on Kraftwerk's 'Trans-Europe Express' with call-and-chant style of James Brown laid over the top. Huge record from New York's Funhouse to Manchester's Haçienda and also the basis for just about every Miami bass record ever.

Although 'Memorabilia' came out as a single, this LP version — with Cindy Ecstasy rapping — is what could probably be described as the first Ecstasy record. Marc Almond and David Ball came across a new drug, MDMA while working in New York and flew over their supplier, Cindy, to perform on the track. If you listen carefully, you can hear "trip, trip, trip" in the background. Despite its age, it still sounds curiously contemporary.

Despite 'Love Can't Turn Around' beating it to the UK pop charts, 'Jack Your Body' was the first no 1 house record, staying there for two weeks at the start of 1987. Given the fact that this was before the mass influx of Ecstasy and the Summers of Love, it's a remarkable testament to the leftfield sensibilities of the general British public that it did so well (and to Pete Tong at London/FFRR who signed it).

An Early Record Sued For Sampling
M/A/R/R/S
'Pump Up The Volume'
(4AD 1987)

The First Acid House Record
Phuture
'Acid Trax'
(Trax 1987)

An Early Techno Record
Rhythim Is Rhythim
'Strings Of Life'
(Transmat/Jack Trax 1988)

The First Big 'Handbag' Record
Black Box
'Ride On Time'
(Deconstruction 1989)

The Quintessential Indie-Dance Tune
Stone Roses
'Fool's Gold'
(Silvertone 1989)

This quirky cut'n'paste dance record was a collaboration between AR Kane and Colourbox with two young DJs, CJ Mackintosh and Dave Dorrell providing the scratching. It spent two weeks at no. 1 in October 1987, but it's real claim to fame was that, along with Coldcut's brilliant remix of 'Paid In Full' by Eric B & Rakim, it kicked off the debate about sampling. This was partly thanks to its judicious use of vocals from James Brown and the aforementioned Eric B, but the really controversial element turned out to be a seven-second wail, sampled from Stock, Aitken & Waterman's smash hit, 'Roadblock'. After SAW sued and won, subsequent copies of the record were released sans-wail and the music industry woke up to sampling.

Teenagers DJ Pierre (aka Nathaniel Jones), Herb Jackson and Spanky (with Marshall Jefferson engineering) came up with this twisted piece of future funk when Pierre discovered that Roland's TR-303 could be mutated into creating haunting arpeggios of bass-notes that rise up and out of the speakers. Originally called 'In Your Mind', they re-named it after people kept walking into record stores and asking for 'Ron Hardy's Acid Track', after the eponymous DJ had been playing it at his club, Music Box. In 1987, this sounded as though it had been beamed down from another planet; nowadays it sounds like the result of a studio full of drugs.

Not the first techno record, but one that suggested that textures and musicality could be as much part of the dance landscape as rhythm. Created by the mercurial DJ Derrick May, it became an M25 rave anthem, loved and played by everyone. Jazzy M recalls playing it at an Energy rave: "The height of the evening was when I played 'Strings Of Life'. Everyone went totally mad. So I stopped it and played it again from the top."

A controversial record in its time thanks to the sample lifted from Loleatta Holloway's 'Love Sensation', which made up the vocal hook. Produced by Daniele Davoli, it kick-started the Italian piano anthem phenomenon and had a big influence on the nascent rave scene. It stayed at no. 1 in the UK chart for six weeks during September and October 1989.

Along with Happy Mondays, Stone Roses were closely associated with the Manchester 'baggy' scene that grew out of the Haçienda's post-acid house period. 'Fool's Gold' was its apotheosis; a shimmering guitar-fuelled piece of funk-rock that sounded as great on a dancefloor as it did on the radio. Popular on both the indie dance circuit and in the Balearic clubs, 'Fool's Gold' made the pop charts twice within a year, in November 1989 and again in September 1990.

An Early Ambient Record
The Orb
'Little Fluffy Clouds'
(Big Life 1990)

A Record To Defy Categorisation
Joey Beltram
'Energy Flash'
(R&S 1991)

An Early Progressive House Record
Gat Decor
'Passion'
(Effective 1992)

An Early Drum And Bass Record
LTJ Bukem
'Demon Theme'
(Good Looking 1992)

A Prototype Big Beat Record
Dust Brothers
'Song To The Siren'
(Junior Boy's Own 1992)

Although ambient had been around in varying forms way before the Orb, this record, which samples Rickie Lee Jones, gave it new meaning just as rave was growing and mutating. Even if it is more ambient house, than actually ambient, it nevertheless captures the essence of what ambient is.

When a teenage kid from Brooklyn put out 'Energy Flash' on a nascent Belgian label known for its hardbeat and fledgling hardcore, it immediately captured everyone's attention — from New York DJs used to spinning deep house, through to DJs like Grooverider on the developing breakbeat scene. A genre-bender of a record, the fact that it could quite easily be categorised as hardcore, house or techno is the key to its wide appeal.

Coined by Mixmag's Dom Phillips in June 1992, the phrase progressive house began as a term of description for new British house productions then emerging, and ended up as a term of abuse for bad records. However, amongst the original progressive records released (generally centred around acts like Leftfield and Slam and labels like Guerrilla), Gat Decor's 'Passion' stands out. Released several times, before becoming a big hit in 1996 with a dreadful version that added the vocal from Degrees of Motion's 'Do You Want It Right Now' to the basic track, it still stands up to scrutiny.

Although it's impossible to pinpoint the start of drum and bass from the proliferation of breakbeat tracks that comprised the hardcore scene of the early-nineties (such as 4 Hero's 'Combat Dancin' or Doc Scott's 'NHS'), LTJ Bukem's third tune, 'Demon Theme' (the first release on his Good Looking label), is as near as any to making a statement of intent, and was a favourite of Fabio and Grooverider at Rage. As Jay, member of bands JMJ & Richie and EZ-Rollers, says, "It opened everyone's minds to what could be done; that you could have musical elements in something that, up until then, had just had cheesy samples".

When two gawky Manchester University graduates recorded a version of Tim Buckley's 'Song To The Siren' (though their version was probably more inspired by This Mortal Coil's ethereal eighties indie version), little did they know they would be setting off a bandwagon's-worth of copyists. Originally released on their own label, Andy Weatherall tipped off Junior Boy's Own about the track which was then licensed to them. Their abrasive mix of classic hip hop breaks with intense keyboard work was the forerunner of much of the so-called big beat style of music.

The Culture

"Why not?" Timothy Leary's final words

"Techno equals death." Madonna

The Politics
of Dancing

…'music' includes sounds wholly or predominantly characterised by the emission of a succession of repetitive beats. Clause 58 (1) (b) Criminal Justice Bill

Dancing is political, stupid.
While you were rolling out of the pub to look for a cash-point and checking the flyer for the DJ line-up, they were asking questions in Parliament about you.

While you were sharing a spliff with some mates after a great Friday night, they were closing down a club because people got high there. While you were sweating up your disco knickers on a podium, loving the attention from the guy in the Moschino top, they were making laws restricting the ways you can legally listen to music.

Today's dance culture started off as a free-wheeling outlaw, running rings around the forces of law and order. Back in the day, dance music was the new punk, a secret soundtrack made in the bedrooms of suburban dub thugs for consumption in all-new rebel celebrations. And if you enjoyed the music the way it was meant to be taken — with a pill rocking your bones from inside your head — you were breaking the law, no doubt about it. Much of what we enjoy now about clubbing grew from unlawful roots, so stop a minute and give thanks to the criminals, the gangsters, the dirty dog-stringing crusties, everyone who ever stuck a finger up at the nation's dance-phobic lawgivers, because without the influence of pirate radio, illegal raves, party-mad travellers and dangerous drugs drugs

drugs, your average weekend entertainment would still be a Malibu and pineapple down at your local Ritzy, listening to hits of the sixties all the way through to as late as midnight.

Clubbing and dance culture is all about large groups of like-minded people, and any time people join together to do something they can't do alone, something that wider society's none too keen about, they're being political. Sure, because drugs are involved as well, it's inevitable that there's government concern, some interest from the powers that be but, even without the added illegality of pills, powder and puff, dancing is an act of rebellion. Whenever you throw off the constraints of daytime life and escape to another world, you are questioning the rules, even if you don't watch the news and you never voted in your life.

The first law specifically targeting dance culture was Graham Bright's 1990 Entertainments (Increased Penalties) Act, which increased the maximum fine for an unlicensed party from £2,000 to £20,000 and six months imprisonment. This was passed as a knee-jerk Tory reaction to 1989's wave of huge illegal acid house raves — parties described in tabloid horror as Ecstasy orgies thrown by wide-boy promoters who raked in hundreds of thousands of pounds. Bright's law was extremely successful in curtailing the rave phenomenon (following a series of busts and mass arrests), but its long term effect, as it forced the growing scene into properly licensed premises, was to encourage councils to grant clubs later licenses and to bring Ecstasy into the mainstream.

There are always people who want to do something just because they've been told 'No', and now that raves had been made more clearly illegal, those sections of the great unwashed who thrived on opposition to the establishment — travellers, pagans, squatters, eco-warriors — decided that throwing free parties, the bigger the better, as a continuation of the old hippie festivals, should now be their main aim. There followed some summer cat-and-mouse madness as the cops and the travellers played tag and, in 1992, when 25,000 people arrived to dance on Castlemorton Common to 100 hours of techno-shamanism from the nation's collected sound systems, the government made it clear that they'd had enough. To set an example, members of the Spiral Tribe sound system were arrested and charged with "conspiracy to cause a public nuisance", only to win their freedom in a court case which cost the taxpayer £4m. In frustration, John Major's government floored the gas pedal on the passing of their hot new item, The Criminal Justice Bill, a wide-sweeping set of laws which amongst other things overturned the centuries-old rights to free assembly and greatly increased the powers of the police. The Criminal Justice Bill was an attempt to fight social change with the iron heel of legislation, and it united the outlaws as never before. The cunning of the young and unemployed was unified as travellers, squatters and protesters all became targets of a single piece of law. Their reaction was swift. You might not have noticed, you probably didn't care, but through these dark days the rebels were out there fighting for your right to party. Most notable was Advance Party, a coalition of sound systems and civil liberties groups who did what they could to bring down the Bill. In the end, however, after some lively showdowns, in 1994 it became law.

The CJB was unique in that it was the first time the pop music of a youth culture had been specifically prohibited. The famous definition of house and techno it contained ("…'music' includes sounds wholly or predominantly characterised by the emission of a succession of repetitive beats") showed just how seriously government saw the threat of dance culture, with its combination of music, drugs and hordes of lusty young people. The aspiring UK police state had outlawed us getting together to have a dance.

For what happened next, you have to slap the back of a policeman. It is really down to the social sensitivity and common sense of the police (!) that the Criminal Justice Act didn't bite as bad as we feared. PC Plod, or at least his chief constable, knew it was pointless to fight against what had become a way of life. Even the drugs thing, the central reason for all this fuss, wasn't something they felt they could just beat with the CJA's hammer. At the end of the century, our society has grudgingly accepted drug culture. Drugs are such a commonplace part of life that it's easy to forget that they are still illegal. The cops knew this and instead of slamming us all in jail, they have increasingly replaced arrests with cautions and adopted a "softly-softly" approach to recreational drug use. Many senior policemen have even admitted that decriminalising soft drugs would probably be a better way of fighting their influence than lumping them together with heroin and crack.

The effect on mass gatherings was a little more severe, and here the police did try out some of their new powers, especially where anti-roads protesters were busy tunnelling against tarmac, but the biggest effect on the raves was simply that the party zone moved from the south into the midlands as rave organisers figured which police forces were most likely to leave them alone. Anyhow, by the time the CJB was law, dance culture had become so mainstream that big underground raves had started to feel like a thing of the past.

And this is the real lasting outcome of the govt vs dance title bout. The establishment couldn't stifle the culture, so instead it forced it into the mainstream. We can thank the law as much as the outlaws for bringing this underground way of partying into the light. They couldn't shut down the dance, so they licensed it and let us free, but in the process they pushed everything into a much less exciting arena: a process which looks likely to continue.

The latest piece of legislation targeting clubbers is Barry Legg's 1997 Public Entertainments Licenses (Drug Misuse) Act, which has made it remarkably easy for local councils to close clubs down if the police suspect drugs are being sold or used on the premises. "Everyone knows clubs and drugs are bedfellows," argued Legg. "What I am hoping to do is make this complacency unacceptable." This crystallised a problem that clubs have always wrestled with: they know that drugs make for a better party, but they know that condoning criminal activity is risking closure. The real power of Legg's law lies in frightening club owners into playing safe, emphasising safe mainstream nights which

don't run the same risks as drug-friendly underground-style events.

However, there is no doubt that the force of this dynamic youth culture has made a huge difference to society. Legg's law is a direct response to the fact that because thousands of people want to have fun together every week, our country is now far more accepting of a sub-culture based on taking drugs and dancing all night. So maybe it was all a little more than just a party. Throughout the eighties, young people were criticised by their radical elders for being apathetic and apolitical, but perhaps the mass movement of dance culture was their answer to a need to unite. Thatcher said, "There is no society," but in her face there were thousands of people making alternative one-night communities. They didn't want to join unions, they didn't want to demonstrate, but they definitely wanted to be together. Even though some of its results — superclubs, millionaire drug cartels and the like — seem hopelessly Thatcherite, dance culture brought us together in a way that no party politics could.

It may not be a deep dark secret any more, the days are gone when you could set up a massive sound system in a field and create a spontaneous party encampment, but instead most weekends near where you live, you can go hear a world-class DJ, you can dance well past the time the pubs shut, and, if you want, you don't have to look far for illegal drugs to heighten the experience. Despite some serious efforts to control them, repetitive beats lie undefeated.

My greatest Ministry moment was probably sitting in the cinema with my girlfriend seeing our **Use Your Vote** advert and knowing that it was in cinemas nationwide.

I came down to the club one night and there was this guy having photographs taken. The following week there was a picture in the newspaper which said "MP outside the Ministry of Sound". I called up his office and said, "If you're really interested in young people's issues why don't you engage us in the process instead of just using us as a credible background for a photocall?"

When he came to the club it started this huge political debate in the office. Some people said "Oh voting's a complete waste of time," but others said, "Well actually my grandfather died to give you the right to vote," or, "In the country I came from I couldn't even vote if I wanted to." Everyone decided we should do something about it.

The first ad we made was banned. It showed a young kid on a hunt with his family and he shoots this deer in the head and then he says "Jolly good kill!" and up came the line 'Use Your Vote, You Know He'll Use His'. It was so powerful, that when I showed it to the International Fund for Wildlife, they agreed to fund the whole campaign.

This was the first time we went really public in saying clubbing is not just about music. There is a huge generation gap at the moment, more extreme than it's ever been, so there are very few people talking on behalf of the two million or so young people that go clubbing each weekend, and yet I honestly think dance culture plays a huge part in people's lives. People see Ministry of Sound as an organisation that's run by young people who talk in their language, so when we do something like this, it's not the government or the council telling them to vote, instead we get respect for who we are, speaking to them in a language they understand.

Mark Rodol, Director, Ministry of Sound.

Use

Your

Vote

USE YOUR VOTE.
YOU KNOW HE'LL USE HIS.

Nightlife's Day Job

Visiting the Ministry of Sound in the daytime can be an unusual experience. Today looks like trouble: there's a police car blocking the entrance. Hordes of middle-aged people in suits are pouring out of the club and the cops are eyeing them as if these businessfolk were a dangerous gang of hooligans. A big club bust? Bossman, James Palumbo, brawling with his investors?

What makes the scene really strange is that the police car in question is of the New York variety, complete with uniformed NYPD police officers, all in Gaunt Street, a stone's throw from the Elephant and Castle and south London's pinkest shopping centre. And now, just to add to the drama, a yellow cab straight from 12th and Broadway drives up onto the pavement, its driver chewing on a cigar and shouting in a Brooklyn accent. "It's a film launch party," says James Bethell, the club's Media Director, as if such things happen every day.

Inside, the club's office, a huge white-washed warehouse, is filled with scurrying young people. They look like clubbers who forgot to go home, all dressed in stylish streetwear and none older than the people who fill the place at the weekend. Maybe working here is like Logan's Run and they kill you when you hit thirty. Over on one side are the people putting together the Ministry magazine. There are glamorous layouts on computer screens, piles of photos spilling everywhere and a diagram on the wall of next month's contents. "Do you like our dildo forest?" asks Pauline, the editor, pointing at a garden of sex-toys growing happily on the top of a computer. "It's in the next issue."

Yasmin and Tanya talk me through the Ministry's fashion and merchandise operation. They show me next season's t-shirt logos — all sweetshop colours and Frisky babies — and some rather natty mobile phone covers they've just had made. Tanya tells me how great it is to be part of a company that's so well known across the globe. "I met this fifty-year old company director in Canada and when I said I worked for Ministry he just said 'Cool!'"

Will shows me the club's website and we chat online for a while, laughing at a few bizarre clubbing stories from the world's websurfers. Behind us, the graphics boys are busy putting together next month's flyers. Back down in the main office there are weekend coaches being booked to bring clubbers from across the country, record deals being signed, tours and nights across the UK and throughout the five continents being organised, and — in the swankier offices — the kind of big-buck deals being struck that you'd expect of one of the country's fastest growing leisure companies. In just a few hours, however, the action will shift to the other side of the building. Past the coffee machine, through the cow-coloured door there will be a thousand clubbers doing their best to destroy the place.

Tonight it will go like this. Around 9pm Nodd, the club manager will arrive and start the long process of preparing the club for opening. He describes himself as 'the grease monkey'. "If something needs a bit of fairy dust on it or a drop of oil to keep the wheels turning, that's where you'll find me. If everything goes perfectly I'd have nothing to do all night," he says. "I'd get bored and go home."

Between ten and eleven the staff will start to drift in, beers will go in the fridge, the ice will arrive, and Nodd will go round checking every detail, heading off potential disasters before the club is filled with inebriated groovers. The first thing he'll check will be the sound system, making sure it's warmed up and humming happily. It's always switched on hours before the club opens and then left on throughout the weekend. In fact, in the winter the mighty boom-box is left on all the time. Amplifiers prefer to have a constant relationship with the world. "It's like a Formula One car," explains Nodd. "If we change the spark plugs we'd have to retune the whole thing." Apart from the amplifiers, the rest of the systems will be booted up, making sure the computers are twinkling, ready to drive the lights, and that the cash registers are ready to swallow people's money.

An hour before showdown, the rest of the gang will start arriving, bar staff will wander in, busboys, cloakroom attendants, toilet attendants, the box-office people, security, the paramedic with his fluorescent band-aids. On a typical night there are about fifty people working in the Ministry.

As opening time grows nearer, the folk known as the 'star squad' will arrive: the guest list person, the picker, the promotions people for the night. Bit by bit the club will be gradually preened and polished until it opens and the first wave of customers flood in. In London, clubs that are open at midnight will close at either 3 or 6am; Ministry of Sound is the only legal place that stays open from midnight until 9am. This means that the club welcomes its punters in waves, first at pub chucking-out time and then as other clubs close. The first wave will go in around midnight, these they call the light-weights. They're mostly gone again by 3am. As these folk are leaving, the more serious clubbers will start to arrive, and then, at four or five in the morning the night-shift, the real professionals, will begin turning up.

So from midnight tonight, it will be open. The rest, if you've been to the club, you know. There'll be top DJs, quality music, drinks, dancing, girls, boys, that kind of thing. And then at the end of the night, the last punters will shuffle out, the lights will be flicked off, the street will be swept and the office next door will start filling up again as the day staff come back to organise the next night of extravagant entertainment.

It can go horribly wrong of course. Justin, the promoter for Saturday's Rulin', remembers one Boxing Day when only 326 people turned up. They had to move them into the VIP room and cancel the great Tony Humphries who was booked to play. "That was the biggest disaster I've seen in here," he laughs.

To Nodd, a disaster means something else. "We've had floods, power failures, collapsing entrance walkways, mystery sneezing ailments working through the whole club," he recalls. "It's surprising the amount of stuff that goes wrong. On one particular night I'd no sooner mopped up a flood than the power failed and I lost the safe key… all in the space of about ten minutes." Power failures are no problem though, as the club can take in juice from about six separate supplies. "We can get electricity from one substation on one side of the building or from another on the other so it's possible for us to borrow from one side to pay the other," he explains. "Quite often had it not been for a couple of hundred metres of cable and a roll of gaffer tape, we wouldn't have been able to open."

Today, all this excitement is yet to come. It's still only after lunch and the club is sitting empty. There are cables and stepladders on the dancefloor, James, the light-man, is checking some bulbs in the bar, Santi, the sound engineer, is showing off the famous system. I ask him to describe it and he blinds me with science, losing me completely when he gets to the bit about the equaliser that uses a radio transmitter which works in MIDI connected to the signals they use for synchronising video playback which lets him adjust something from the middle of the room. Instead of bluffing my way in MIDI, I ask him who was the most demanding DJ, knowing full well that he's going to say Junior Vasquez. Which he does.

He won't say how many watts the box pumps, only that you can turn it up louder than Concorde. He shows me the amplifiers in their upstairs cupboard and there's a digital read-out which says 'FUCKING LOUD'.

Santi has to go and fetch something, leaving me alone in the booth. I press the start button on one of the four decks but there are no records around. My Ministry debut will have to wait a little longer. Instead, I wander to the centre of the room

and tap my toes a little. Clubs in the daytime aren't quite real. You can see all the scuffs and the scratches, the lights are bright and boring, and without people and music it seems like the skeleton of something dead. I wonder why the babes are avoiding me, why I can't hear the music, why I can't find my mates on the dancefloor. It's almost a shame to see one of the world's greatest rooms looking like nothing more than an empty black warehouse with some speaker stacks in it. When the sound is sleeping you can hear the trains rumble overhead.

The
Economics
of Clubbing

"Sorted!"
This is not the grunt of a sweaty 'ardkore 'ead, twitching his white gloves in the strobe. It's an advert from the Post Office, the venerable Royal Mail, established 1635. **Since when did Postman Pat steal the slang of the E generation?**

Since he realised that's who's got the spending power these days, that's when. Want to track down some young people? They won't be at home watching TV, they probably won't be sitting in a murky pub — they'll be out larging it on the dancefloor. Two-thirds of 18–24 year-olds club at least once a month, nearly a third go every week. And since clubbers spend nearly 20% more cash than Miss and Mr Average, big businesses are falling over each other in their attempts to speak our language. To them you might be a 'Lad Lauren', a 'Gill and Ted', an 'Educated Hedonist' or perhaps a 'Rough Guide Professional'; just four of nine 'typologies' identified by youth market researchers ROAR to help the big companies dig for your dollars. These categories are all about how you spend your spare time, what television you watch, where you go out, what magazines you read and of course — how you splash your cash. And whether you're a 'Play-Safe Careerist' ("cautious, hardworking and conscious of the need to provide for their future") or a 'Cool Britannia' ("often first into new trends"), you're also a target. It's not just about the amount of disposable dosh you have, it's also — hold onto your

hats — that people who go clubbing are far more sophisticated, intelligent and discerning, the kind of consumers who are the most valuable to marketeers. To flash a bit more jargon, you are more likely to be what they call an 'early adopter', an 'opinion former', and 'self-directed'. You are open to new experiences and you are likely to be ahead of the pack. Also, when you find something good, you tell your mates about it. You care about what labels you wear, what brands you buy, you get a kick out of clever commercials, and have a lot of influence. Pat yourself on the back.
All this is what explains the rushing techno soundtracks and shiny clubwear babes in TV advertising, the strangely incongruous graphic emphasis of the letter E in certain print ads, and the 'repositioning' of long-established brands (post-clubbing cornflakes anyone?). Even book publishing, one of the most conservative industries, has caught onto the power of using club culture to reach trendy twentysomethings. Irvine Welsh showed them that people who go to clubs can also manage to read a book, and ever since, bookstores have been crammed with fluorescent book jackets and flyer-type graphics — Alcopop fiction! We've got a culture and they're gonna use it.
However, it is alcopops themselves which are the most obvious reaction to the rise and rise of club culture. The brewing industry had already suffered a mass exodus from the pubs, and freaked when they saw how the popularity of illegal drugs had put them in direct competition with something as cost-effective and powerfully marketed as Ecstasy. If booze was to fight back it had to somehow become potent, colourful, young. It had to battle to be a major part of the club experience against a psychedelic pill with a cartoon character on it. Meet Hooch and his mates. Fruit-

flavoured alcoholic beverages became one of the fastest-established new product sectors ever.
But if you're marketing to young clubbers, you'd better get it right. No-one likes to think that their culture has been stolen and abused to sell them something. "Young people are incredibly intelligent and they're cynical of the motives behind advertising," says VJ Anand, the UK Promotions Manager of Ericsson mobile phones. "That's why we market with respect. We don't want to shove the phone down peoples throats… we just want to put some money back into the underground and say thank you to the DJs." Whether you believe such altruism, sponsorship is one way advertisers can reach you while you're clubbing, another is by 'sampling' — offering you a free try of a new product. Trade magazine Precision Marketing recommends this to its readers: "If a brand can make it onto the table during a night out, there is a strong chance it will be adopted as part of the clubber's normal repertoire." So that explains the people wandering round clubs giving out packets of cigarettes and dodgy new drinks for free. In the end, it's all a sign of the influence you've got. Ever since they invented the teenager back in the fifties, young people have been the key to successful marketing: catch them young and keep them coming back. Club culture is the dominant form of entertainment for young people today and it's increasingly the heart of our identities. In the UK alone, clubbing is a multi-billion-pound business, and because it's worth so much money, it's completely changing the rules of this glittering consumerist world in which we live, die and shop. Fuck! How did I spend that much tonight? Not even enough left to buy some orange juice and Rizlas on the way home.

The Ministry of Economic Success

Walk into the offices of the Ministry of Sound and the first thing you see, amongst the framed posters and gold discs, is a declaration of the club's mission:

"We are building a global entertainment business based on a strong aspirational brand, respected for its creativity and quality. The Ministry of Sound team will be more professional, hard-working and innovative than any other on the planet."

We are building a global entertainment business, based on a strong aspirational brand, respec for its creativity and qua

The Ministry of Sound t will be more profession hard-working and innov than any other on the pl

It's easy to play the fiercely underground clubber and sneer at such an ambitious business doctrine. You might see it as the megalomania of a corporate superclub — 'The Misery', the McDonalds of dance culture, but this businesslike attitude has made the Ministry of Sound the most famous club in the world and one of the most successful of all time.

This year there will be hundreds of Ministry of Sound events across the globe, from New York to China to Ibiza to Nigeria. You can hear music from the Ministry on radio stations across the world, or on the Internet where there's a busy Website. You can buy Ministry magazine, records on their MOS and Open labels, one of their hugely successful compilation CDs, or something from a vast range of clothing and merchandise. If you're caught thirsty inside the club you can even buy the Ministry's own brand of bottled water. "Ministry is not run as a traditional club," explains Director Mark Rodol, "It's run along the basis that we're a funky youth brand and one of our outlets happens to be a club." In fact, though it takes the bulk of the organisation's time and effort to run, in terms of revenue, the club is down at the bottom of the list of earners, with the record label and merchandise at the top. "It makes no commercial sense whatsoever, the amount of time we agonize over the club. But I wouldn't like to run the record label without having the club, I wouldn't like to do the magazine or the clothing business without having the club. It's still the most important thing we do and it always will be."

The Ministry is proud of breaking new ground, of testing how far they can push the influence of a mere nightclub. This tactic often upsets the dance community, but usually proves itself to be foresight as much as arrogant commercialism. When they announced in 1994 that Pepsi were to sponsor their club tour, this radical move was met by outrage, but a few years later, as Rodol points out "If you look at the club ads it's easier to ask who isn't sponsored." He looks to the success of a company like Virgin as a model for the Ministry's future. "Virgin are now flying planes across to America, 20 years ago they were a basement record label in Notting Hill or somewhere. The most exciting thing about Ministry is we still don't know how far can we take it."

At its most mundane, Ministry of Sound is a club in south London. At its most exalted — because of its economic clout and its power as a brand name — it is an organisation that strives to give dance culture a unified and marketable face. Ministry is, of all things, a club that has fans — just like a pop band. "Dance music is the biggest collaboration of young people since the sixties," argues Rodol, "and yet dance culture is very faceless. If you're into dance music and the whole culture of dance, and the whole lifestyle, then who do you follow? You follow Ministry of Sound."

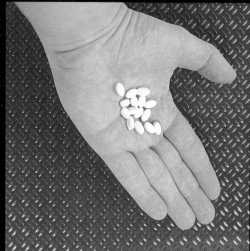

87

Ten years
of clubbing

DJs return from Ibiza with
the idea for a new way of
doing things.
Delirium at Heaven with
Noel Watson.
The Ramplings start Shoom.
Trevor Fung spins balearic
at The Project.
Jazzy M champions house
on Jacking Zone show
on LWR.
Troll at Soundshaft.
The cast of Grange Hill
release their 'Just Say No'
anti-drugs record.

Tunes
Steve Silk Hurley
'Jack Your Body'
SAW 'Roadblock'
M/A/R/R/S
'Pump Up The Volume'

Real Life
Black Monday brings
eighties greed-culture
crashing down.
The Sun write a story
about finding 25,000
'Ecstasy wrappers' on the
ground after a rave.
Margaret Thatcher is
elected to a third term as
Prime Minister.

SCO

88

89

Smileys everywhere as Spectrum and Shoom take house and Ecstasy to an eager public.
Headlines like 'Shoot These Evil Acid Barons' and 'Acid Rock Records Banned By The Beeb' show just how wrong the tabloids can be.
Graeme Park starts a residency at Manchester's Haçienda.
The idea of large scale raves starts with events like Sunrise.
The Akai 1000 sampler is released, music-making technology on a bedroom scale.
Fashion: Fluorescent clothes, bandannas and dungarees.

Tunes
Guy Called Gerald 'Voodoo Ray'
Royal House 'Can You Party'
Jolly Roger 'Acid Man'
D-Mob 'We Call It Acieed'
Inner City 'Big Fun/Good Life'

Real Life
All-day drinking introduced in England and Wales.
M25 completed.
George Bush elected US President.
Mikhail Gorbachev becomes Soviet President.
Terrorist bomb explodes Pan Am jumbo jet over Lockerbie.
Thatcher invents the poll tax

Raves get bigger and bigger as canny promoters smell money.
Thousands drive round the M25 in search of fun: Biology, Sunrise, Energy…
Madchester makes everything floppy as Inspiral Carpets, Happy Mondays, Stone Roses weld guitar band traditions to the new dance styles.
Kate Moss debuts.
The rise of Acid Jazz with clubs like Gilles Peterson's Talkin' Loud all-dayers at Dingwalls.
House sound systems appear at the Glastonbury festival for the first time.
Ambient house is born as the Orb and KLF release

New Order's 'Technique' LP, an ironic comment on Ecstasy and Ibiza, is their most successful to date.
Cyberculture begins to appear as bedroom boffins realise that technology can be cool.
Fashion: Kickers, hoodies and long hair.

Tunes
Lil' Louis 'French Kiss'
Rhythim Is Rhythim 'Strings Of Life'
808 State 'Pacific State'
Soul II Soul 'Keep On Moving'
Black Box 'Ride On Time'

Real Life
Germany reunified and

Romanian u
Green party
the vote in E
Police worr
in the UK.
Student loa
Hillsboroug
ninety-five d
death at foc
in Sheffield

90

91

Madchester climaxes with Happy Mondays' 'Pills Thrills And Bellyaches' and the Stone Roses concert on Spike Island. Guns and gangsterism kill the vibe soon afterwards.
The idea of taking the fun of the club to the beach begins as Ibiza reunions become popular.
Sheffield's Warp Records promotes the rise of bleepy techno music.
Fashion: Red jeans, long-sleeved T-shirts and Italian football tops.

Tunes
Primal Scream 'Loaded'
Xpansions 'Elevation'
Deee-Lite
'Groove Is In The Heart'
Orbital 'Chime'
LFO 'LFO'

Real Life
Hurricanes kill forty-four people in southern England. Saddam Hussein invades Kuwait and the US responds. Margaret Thatcher resigns as PM and is replaced by John Major.
Reunification treaty signed between East and West Germany.
Anti Poll Tax demonstration in Trafalgar Square becomes the largest riot in London's history.

A super-successful year for rave with massive legal events like Raindance and World Party.
The scene begins to split, with hardcore venturing off into the underground and house going into clubs nationwide.
The Ministry of Sound opens, bringing top US DJs over and offering a true New York experience to London.
In Stoke, a club called Shelley's opens and a DJ called Sasha wows the crowds there.
Hardcore loonies like Prodigy and Altern 8 rise from the raves.
"Nice one, top one, sorted" Lightsticks, whistles, tambourines and white gloves.

Italian piano tracks.
The KLF make much money with a series of arty jokes which are actually hit singles.

Tunes
Massive Attack
'Unfinished Sympathy'
Sounds Of Blackness
'The Pressure'
K-Klass
'Rhythm Is A Mystery'
Moby 'Go'
Bizarre Inc
'Playing With Knives'

Real Life
Gulf War as America attacks Iraqi forces.
IRA mortar bomb the garden of 10 Downing St.
Yugoslavia erupts in civil war; Serbs vs Croats.
Robert Maxwell's body found floating in the Atlantic. A military coup in the Soviet Union; Boris Yeltsin becomes president.

92

93

The Daily Star declares that the nation is 'In The Grip Of E' (in letters up to six inches high) asserting that more than half a million kids are 'hooked on the mind-bending drug'. Underworld take techno to the stage at Glastonbury. Clubbing goes Glam as the Ramplings open the club of the same name, insisting on a strict 'dress-up-or-go-home' door policy. Kinky Gerlinky, Pussy Galore and Pushca do the same.

In Leeds, Back II Basics is born.

Castlemorton, a huge free party created by the concerted effort of several itinerant sound systems, notably Spiral Tribe, is the culmination of the travellers' movement, the crusty combination of techno and gypsy life.

Tunes

Gat Decor 'Passion'
Future Sound Of London 'Papua New Guinea'
Degrees Of Motion 'Do You Want It Right Now'
DOP 'Groovy Beat'
D:Ream 'UR The Best Thing'

Real Life

Los Angeles riots, sparked by the beating of Rodney King. 44 people die.
Black Wednesday, the latest financial crash.
Bill Clinton defeats George Bush to become President of the USA.

Despite high hopes for Labour, the Conservatives win a record-breaking fourth term in the general election.

Techno, long ridiculed by journos, rises again as complex jazz ideas, mystical Detroit figures and fantastic records come to the fore. The trendies respond by calling it 'intelligent' techno. Meanwhile, Belgians and Germans are using Hoover noises and stompy beats to invent trance.

The Criminal Justice & Public Order Bill is the first law to specifically outlaw a type of music, 'defined wholly or partially by a succession of repetitive beats'. Opposition groups rally against this threat to our freedom to party.

The Drum Club is London's place to be.
Hard house begins to flow from New York, notably Junior Vasquez's Sound Factory sound.

Gay and straight clubbers find it a lot easier to dance in the same place as clubs like Leeds' Vague redefine things.

Tunes

Leftfield/Lydon 'Open Up'
X-Press 2 'Music X-Press'
Mariah Carey 'Dream Lover'
Jaydee 'Plastic Dreams'
M-People 'Movin' On Up'

Real Life

FBI storm cult of David Koresh in Waco, Texas.
Israel and the PLO sign a peace deal.
South Africa ratifies a democratic constitution.
IRA bomb kills two children in Warrington.

94

95

Glamour clubbing turns into sexy clubbing, and flyers become full of nudity. The Heavenly Social launches the Chemical (née Dust) Brothers and the new spirit of anything goes — including guitars, old-skool rap and the Beatles — creates dance music for people who don't dance.

Jungle emerges from the rave underground through pirate radio and clubs like AWOL, Rage and Roast to become the soundtrack for the summer.

Fashion: Baby doll dresses and shiny shirts.

Tunes
Paperclip People 'Throw'
Goldie 'Inner City Life'
Billy Ray Martin
'Your Loving Arms'
Leviticus 'Burial'
MD Express
'God Made Me Funky'

Real Life
Serial killers Fred and Rose West are arrested. Rwandan civil war brings half a million deaths. Nelson Mandela is inaugurated as the president of South Africa. IRA declare a ceasefire in Northern Ireland. UK National Lottery is launched.

The rise and rise of superclubs Cream, Renaissance, Ministry. Serious clubbers react against handbag house. Ministry of Sound takes clubbing on tour, sponsored by Pepsi.

Danny Rampling gets a Radio 1 show.
Goa trance.
Vasquez-mania.
Universe join forces with Mean Fidler to throw Tribal Gathering.
LTJ Bukem's club, Speed, takes drum and bass to the trendsters.
The irresistible rise of Oasis begins.
Fashion: Anoraks and

Tunes
Bucketheads 'The Bomb'
Wink 'Higher State Of Consciousness'
DeLacey 'Hideaway'
Jamiroquai
'Space Cowboy'
Alcatraz 'Giv Me Luv'

Real Life
Barings Bank collapses.
Bombing of Oklahoma Federal Building kills 168.
OJ Simpson gets off.
Israeli PM Yitzhak Rabin assassinated.
Bosnian peace treaty signed.

96

97

BMA warns that Ecstasy could cause long-term brain damage.
Barry Legg introduces the Public Entertainments Licences Drugs Misuse Act, allowing local authorities to close clubs if police suspect drugs are taken there.
Sex Pistols reform for a live tour, the first in eighteen years.
Jarvis Cocker humiliates Jacko at the Brit awards.
Take That split.
Prodigy amaze by becoming enduring pop stars with chart hits like 'Firestarter'.
Bjork is sent an acid bomb by an obsessed fan.
Rappers Tupac and Notorious BIG are shot dead.
Fashion: Nikes and baggy combat trousers.

Tunes
Tori Amos
'Professional Widow'
Underworld 'Born Slippy'
BBE 'Seven Days And One Week'
The Fugees 'The Score'
CJ Bolland
'Sugar Is Sweeter'

Real Life
A fire erupts in the Channel Tunnel.
Charles and Diana divorce.
Dunblane massacre.

Doctors identify club-related ailments such as PVC bottom and clubber's nipple.
Daft Punk lead an invasion of French music.
Big Beat label Skint enjoys big success.
Matthew Collins' Altered State is published, the first serious retrospective of the Ecstasy years.
Speed Garage takes the floor, with Rosie Gaines' 'Closer Than Close', and Double 99's 'RIP Groove' in the charts. It's a London thing.
NHS doctors point out that for all the concern over illegal drugs, the biggest causes of club casualties are still booze, bouncers and bottles.

Ibiza enjoys a boom summer revival.
Spice Girls rise, but a fall is (wrongly) predicted after they sack their manager.

Tunes
Daft Punk
'Around The World'
Sneaker Pimps
'Spin Spin Sugar'
Ultra Nate 'Free'
Chemical Brothers
'Block Rockin' Beats'
Roni Size & Reprazent
'Brown Paper Bag'

Real World
Labour win a landslide general election.
Princess Diana dies.
Scotland and Wales vote for devolution.

London is officially the Swinging capital of Cool Britannia.

2020

Future Clubbing

By the year 2020 night-clubs will be completely different.

We will all have to buy special Velcro shoes so that we can go to the Ministry of Sound and, as Lionel Ritchie once put it, dance on the ceiling. As a result of Velcro dancing, people will have thighs like a pair of punchbags and they will rustle together so much that chafing will be endemic.

Money will be abolished, instead we will use micro-chips that look like smiley badges, fitted to the palms of our hands. These will be swiped on an infra-red psycho-active green baize pad at the door of the club which will then automatically debit our accounts. Once inside the club, we will go directly to the changing rooms to change in to our club kit (each club having its own uniform, specially designed in futuristic Crimplene by a leading fashion house such as BHS or C&A) and put on our juice'n'vitamin belts. The vitamin pills will automatically replenish our body when the green indicator — fitted to everybody's left earlobe at birth — turns red while the juice capsules will prevent dehydration. There will also be a space on the belt for potatoes. Not because they're good for you, but because they'd look pretty darn funny.

The effect of having everyone wearing the same uniform will produce a startlingly egalitarian feel to the club; and no longer will girls point and stare at potential love rivals and say, "I don' t know how that fat cow's got the cheek to wear that." In any case, by this time everyone will have reconciled their differences and will live in perfect loving harmony. Apart from hippies, the layabout scum.

Fitted around the edges of the dancefloor will be vending machines, selling 'pulling kits'. These are packs for couples who have just met and want to go back to their underwater jetpad to engage in kinky sex (virginity having been officially outlawed in 2010). Included in the kit will be a toothbrush, toothpaste, condoms, industrial Swarfega, cling film and edible knickers (in three flavours: Pimms No. 1, Trebor's Refreshers and for those no-nonsense couples, Tennent's lager). Promiscuity will be widespread by this time, not because it's so great or anything, but because there'll be nothing else to do. By the vending machines, there will be pumps which, if you swipe your smiley hand over the pad provided, will dispense the latest youth drink craze: Custard-

Shots. These will come in a variety of flavours: chocolate and Creme de Menthe, vanilla and milk stout, or pink and spotted dick.

The music in the club will no longer be provided by a DJ. Everyone will have a button fitted on their trendy saffron, puce and jade tunics and they will be able to send electronic votes through to the computerised DJ console (which will look just like the cockpit in the plane on Airplane except without the blow-up doll). The tracks (or Velcro Grooves as they will be called by then) with the most votes will get ignored whilst the rest will get played, thus carrying on the DJs' tradition of bloody-mindedness.

Toilets won't be needed by the year 2020 because everyone will be fitted with a perspex colostomy globe on their head, with tubes that connect to the relevant region of the body. These will occasionally be emptied by trained Globe Collectors, who are recognisable by their colourful yellow satin all-in-one bodysuits. For relaxation, chill-out rooms manned by trained Brain Chefs, will feed hungry clubbers with specially prepared brain-food, such as mathematical problems, crossword puzzles, chemistry experiments and little kaleidoscopes that show dead neat little coloured patterns that make you go, "Coo".

One thing's for sure: the future's will be so bright you' re going to have to wear underwater goggles.

Michael Alig

Who? As the founder of the notorious Club Kids, Michael Alig was once the king of New York nightlife. **King of New York?** Not the whole city, stupid, just all of it that mattered. **Wall Street? The Upper East Side? Where exactly do you mean?** Well, mostly the back bar in the Limelight. Also Club USA while it lasted, and the Tunnel when it opened the second time around. Oh, and perhaps the Palladium on a good night. **What's a Club Kid?** Hideous freaks, nightbirds of paradise, a bunch of super-weird egomaniac 'gender-fuck' monsters who personified the finest microcelebrity excesses of nineties New York. **Is it drug-related?** Only Valium, cocaine, ketamine, Ecstasy, heroin, crystal and crack, together and in volume. **Sounds great, how many GCSEs do I need?** You just have to be a misfit hick from Bumblefuck Indiana or thereabouts. Everyone at highschool hates you because you're gay/weird/differently-fashionable and/or a second-rate drag queen. As soon as you can scrape together the bus fare, you head for New York, get a glass-collecting job in the Limelight, move into Hotel 17, take lots of hard drugs, and force the world to notice how fabulous you are. Within seconds you'll be a promoter earning big money for filling a club with fellow weirdos, and a few minutes later Ricki Lake or Geraldo will make you their freak of the week, allowing you the perfect revenge on all the trailer-trash thugs who beat you up since kindergarten who are now forced to watch you preen on national network television. **And…?** Oh, don't forget to pierce any body part that didn't come with a hole already in it, put on a lot of white foundation and get a pair of super-high platform trainers. And piss in people's drinks. **Anything else?** Talk about freedom of expression a lot, and how in your club everyone can finally be themselves. **Provided they were born to be pee-drinking, cross-dressing junkies and sexual deviants?** Or pantomime chickens. **Why is he no longer king of New York?** Because The Spice Girls and Howard Stern are. Also because he took too many drugs and murdered his room-mate, a wing-wearing Columbian drug dealer named Angel, for being tacky. **So Michael was never tacky himself?** Not even the time he threw an outlaw party at Burger King in Times Square and wore silver lamé lederhosen with the front cut out, along with a silver-foil penis wrap. **Not the greatest at covering things up then?** After the murder, he bragged to everyone, "Angel was so boring, I had to kill him." Twenty people knew the full story before the police were even interested. **So it was a hopelessly glamorous death, filled with the kind of romantic intricacies beloved of Inspector Morse?** Not really. After bludgeoning Angel with a hammer, Alig smothered him with a pillow, injected him with heroin, poured drain-cleaner down his throat and taped up his mouth, left his body in the bath for a few days, then chopped him up and dumped him in the Hudson River. Allegedly. **He must have been careful moving the body from his apartment?** This is New York remember. He hailed a yellow cab and had the driver help him put the corpse in the trunk. **Not to be confused with…** Michael Palin, Michael Jackson, Kenneth Halliwell. **Most likely to say…** "Come to my sentencing party. Dress as a headless Club Kid, It'll be a scream." **Least likely to say…** "I'd rather stay in tonight and catch Dad's Army."

046

Ambient

Cor, I don't half feel a bit sleepy. That'll be the ambient music you're listening to. **Ambient? What the heck is that?** It's a term coined by ex-Roxy Music man Brian Eno when he released 'Music For Airports' on his own Ambient label in 1978 (Eno also brought this style of music to a much wider audience thanks to his work with Bowie on LPs like 'Heroes' and 'Low'). Although the genre has been around a lot longer than that, managing to survive unhindered for eighty years without a name. **Eighty years?** Yup. The godfather of ambient is Erik Satie, French neo-classical composer, whose 1889 piece 'Trois Gymnopedies' trashed the classical aesthetic with some seriously sparse compositions for piano. They've since been widely utilised in ads and the like. **What's all that got to do with dance music then, squire?** Despite it being championed by Brian Eno, it remained a largely intellectual pursuit, until the quartet of Jimmy Cauty, Bill Drummond (both of the KLF), Alex Patterson (of The Orb) and Youth (from Brilliant) introduced birdsong, whale noises and weirdy-beardy German synthesiser music to the chill-out room at Paul Oakenfold's legendary Land Of Oz acid house shindigs. DJ Mixmaster Morris has also been at the forefront of this electronica revolution **How does one define ambient then?** It's an often (but not always) beatless experience with the emphasis on dreamy textures of keyboards, layered with cosmic samples (often drug or hippy related) and spacey bass notes that combine to provide a futuristic easy listening experience. **So Radio Two for degree-wielding hippie bastards then?** That's about the long and short of it. **How did we get from Erik Satie to acid house?** In the interim, there was the school of experimental American composers like Steve Reich, Terry Riley (no relation to Teddy), Philip Glass and, perhaps the most influential, John Cage, whose 1952 piece '4'33"' was four minutes and thirty-three seconds of silence, perhaps the ultimate ambient music. **The ultimate emperor's new clothes, you mean?**

Easy, fellah. **Well, it sounds pretty bloody dull to me.** In the past ten years, it has developed a surprisingly wide frame of reference with acts like Global Communication, Irresistible Force and Reload, alongside DJs such as the aforementioned Mixmaster Morris and Cafe del Mar's José Padilla. And you're as likely to hear the soundtrack to 'Bullitt' or 'Once Upon A Time In America' as you are the Orb. **Don't suppose you've got a quote from one of these herberts that we can have a good laugh at?** Sure do. Erik Satie said, "Furniture music creates a vibration; it has no other goal; it fills the same role as light and heat — as comfort in every form." **Least likely to say…** "Anarchy in the UK." **Most likely to say…** "Lie down and be counted." **Not to be confused with…** Ambulance, amulet, illbient, ambidextrousness.

I was walking to brunch after a sweaty night at Sound Factory with two queens who were a couple, Michael and Mike. It was nearly winter and I was freezing so I don't know how Mike was surviving because all he had on was a pair of sequinned cycling shorts and this dinky little waistcoat made of ostrich feathers. We were walking past the gas station on 23rd and Tenth when this stretch limo pulled over. The window winds down and this big black gangster says **"How much do you want for the vest?"** (vest is American for waistcoat). Mike told him **"I'm sorry, it's not for sale,"** several times, but the guy got out of the car and started waving a wad of hundred dollar bills. There were two or three girls inside and they were giggling. We were smirking too because this guy was huge and tough and here he was desperately trying to buy the faggiest piece of clothing in New York. Eventually he offered Mike $400 for it and, wetting himself at the situation, too poor to turn down such a ridiculous offer, Mike said yes. He walked to the diner and then home, in November, in nothing but a pair of shorts with a whole month's rent stuffed down the crotch. James Loughton, Designer

The Come-Down

Blimey, I feel terrible. Well, it serves you right young man. Perhaps you'll listen to us next time. **But why do I feel so rotten?** Because you have been taking illegal narcotics which — while they make you run around like a loon for a while telling everyone you love them and that you'll always be their friend — are very bad for you. **But I don't understand. I felt so great last night.** That is the nature of the beast (or, in this case, the beats), dear friend. You have to take the rough with the smooth and what you're feeling now is very much the rough. **But, but... I still really like it.** Well, it's your decision, but don't ever say we didn't warn you. Don't you realise how many people's lives have been ruined by the sort of nefarious activities that you've been getting up to? **How come?** As Arno Adelaars, the Dutch author of a book on Ecstasy, explains: "One of the brain's neuro-transmitters is Serotonin, which takes care of emotional stability. What MDMA does to Serotonin is to boost it, make it fire more rapidly, which produces that euphoric feeling. But in the long term it depletes the supply of Serotonin." It's also been discovered that people who commit suicide usually have extremely low levels of Serotonin. **Alright, keep your hair on. I was only asking.** Ecstasy has also been responsible for a number of deaths, beginning with 16-year-old Claire Leighton, who died in 1989 after buying Ecstasy at the Haçienda, and leading up to high - profile cases such as Leah Betts, who died having collapsed at her 18th birthday party in Latchingdon, Essex on November 16th 1995. Despite this, no-one is exactly sure why some people take lots of drugs with no apparent after-effects, whilst others take one pill and either become very ill or, worse, die. **You're presenting a fairly stark picture of my average Saturday night, if you don't mind me saying, guv'nor.** Well, this generation is effectively the human guinea pig for MDMA testing since so little legally sanctioned research has been done. On May 28th 1994 Dr Charles Grob of the Harbor-UCLA Medical Center in California gave MDMA to a patient, the first legal prescription of it since it was made illegal. Although his experiments were not based on recreational use, he came to two key conclusions: one, that it caused a small increase in body temperature and; two, that it raised blood pressure, albeit minimally. Don't forget, also, that Ecstasy is illegal — has been since 1977 in the UK — and is classified as a Class A drug under the Misuse Of Drugs Act. **I suppose you're recommending that I don't take any artificial stimulants ever again?** Well, it's down to you, sunshine. The facts are that hundreds of thousands of people indulge themselves every weekend and the majority appear to come out unscathed, whilst a tiny minority suffer as a result of it. Whatever, by taking Ecstasy you are breaking the law and submitting yourself to a giant experiment, the results of which probably won't be known for decades. **Most likely to say...** "I can't make it into work today. I've got the 'flu." **Least likely to say...** "Fancy another cheeky half?" **Not to be confused with...** Come Dancing, 'Come All Ye Faithful', Watership Down.

At the opening party for Twilo I found myself dancing next to this guy who thought he was a rock star and some blonde midget who was squeezed into this lace-up PVC number three sizes too small. I knew that it was someone famous but I was in no fit state to recognise her. Finally I realized it was Kimberley out of Neighbours. I told everyone the next day, hoping they'd be impressed, but they put me straight. **It was Pamela Anderson.** Simon Das, clubber

When I saw how many people were going out at twelve o'clock at night. And paying five dollars for a Coca-Cola and five dollars for admission! And I had a restaurant and I would get thirty-five cents for a Coke and they would scream and yell that it was too much money… **I said what the hell am I doing? I should be doing what they're doing.**

Maurice Brahms, New York club owner

I teach five and six-year-old kids in North London. One day we were measuring various things on these scales when this little kid piped up: **"My dad has a pair of scales like those, Miss. He weighs this white powder stuff on them."** I told him it was perhaps best if he didn't repeat this piece of information to anyone else. Madeleine Smith, teacher

Drum and Bass

Three syllables, sounds like…? A hip hop breakbeat spirals into an unfeasibly fast tempo, scattering a ballistic spray of snare drums over the crowd; a dub-speed sub-bass explosion falls out of the mix, leaving a crater in the dancefloor; a wave of soothing jazzy vocals weaves around for a bit, and then the sonic onslaught returns. **Ahh, jungle!** No, drum and bass. **Jam and bass?** No, drum and bass: music characterised by a frenetic snare drum pattern derived from an accelerated break-beat sample, combined with a synthesised sub-bass bassline reminiscent of ragga and a sampled melody from a jazz, R&B or garage source, often created using timestretching techniques. **Surely you mean jungle.** No, no, no. Drum and bass is completely different. **How?** Well drum and bass is intellectual music. It's all about recontextualisation, about post-modern urban blues, about deconstructing rhythm, about… **Oh, jungle for students.** Exactly. And media people too. **So… who invented it?** Jungle was the bastard offspring of hip hop and hardcore techno, with a few important elements of Jamaican ragga thrown in for good measure. It emerged in the early-nineties as techno producers began including breakbeats in their records. Reggae-style toasting became an important part of the genre, it was fostered by pirate radio, and although the connection is sometimes overstated, the music evolved within the background of the growing UK crack underworld. **Why is it so important?** Because it was the UK's first truly indigenous form of Black music. **Indigenous?** Jungle in the UK is like hip hop in the US. British listeners can feel proud that it is a product of their time and place, (unlike hip hop which was always a cultural import). **OK, so that's jungle, but who invented drum and bass?** A lot of journalists who wanted to hide from the fact that they'd been slagging off jungle for years. **I hear David Bowie has a lot to do with it.** No comment. **What about this Goldie fellow?** The first star of jungle… sorry, drum and bass. **So what's Big Beat?** Well that's just hip hop but for students. **And Speed Garage?** That's drum and bass but for girls. **Not to be confused with…** Drum and bag, Mama Cass, fife and drum. **Really not to be confused with…** Jungle. **Most likely to say…** A splendid re-appropriation of the spatiality of jazz fusion. **Least likely to say…** Wicked! **So what's timestretching?** Speeding something up. It's very complicated.

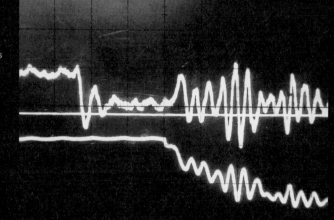

Some mates went to The Camden Palace but the doormen wouldn't let them in. They decided the best approach was to be polite and persistent and they explained that, yes, they were a little drunk and, yes, they weren't with any girls, but they were dressed really smart and they'd come a long way and, most importantly of all, they went there every Friday, always had a great time and had never had trouble getting in before. The bouncer listened sympathetically, considered their tale of woe, then said, **"The problem is: today's Saturday. So fuck off."** Ian Regis, carpenter

052

A girlfriend of mine turned up at the Ministry with four other blondes and a brunette. **The brunette told the bouncers she was the manager and the rest were a Belgian girl band called Dies** (pronounced Dee-ez) **on a reccy for their first gig in the UK. Having proffered the requisite big smiles and "ya's" to every question, they were given VIP passes and had an extremely good night.** Shaun Harley, journalist

Garage

Born... Mid-eighties. **That's a bit of a funny word for a type of music isn't it?** Well, it's essentially music that used to be played at the Garage. **What, you mean like the bus garage?** No, you fool. It's pronounced Gar-aahj, rather than the British Gar-ijj. The Paradise Garage was a club in New York where DJ Larry Levan was resident. He played an intense brew of classic disco and electronic sounds, with a smattering of funky rock records. **So that's what garage is then?** Well, here's the funny thing. Garage nowadays is taken to mean an uplifting vocal track with the accent on melody and soul; an update of the disco sound of the late-seventies/early-eighties. Music with a message (and that message is 'lurve'). Which is but one of the styles that Levan played at the Garage. **Why's it called garage then?** Why's a biscuit called a cookie? Why's a spade not a shovel? How do we know. Journalists need catch-all phrases and garage is as good as any. **But that's not what Ashley Beedle thinks is it?** Er, no: "There's been this kind of up-your-own-arse garage game, where we call it garage music. But it's not garage music at all. Calling this stuff that comes out now garage music is a fallacy. It's more akin to the New Jersey sound. If you want to call it anything, call it club or New Jersey or even the Zanzibar sound." **So when did disco start being garage then? Was there a party to celebrate the changeover?** Now you're being immature. It wasn't a relay race with baton change, you know. As electronic instruments were coming on to the market, so disco began to mutate from its traditional live sound with orchestral productions, into the more urban electronic sound. Early records like Peech Boys' 'Don't Make Me Wait' (incidentally the first record to include an a cappella), utilised these machines to create modern soul. **Who invented it then?** Nobody and several. The aforementioned Peech Boys were produced by Levan; François Kevorkian's mixes of D-Train influenced its progress; New Jersey's Paul Simpson with

productions such as Serious Intention's 'You Don't Know' on Easy Street led the way; whilst another New Jersey outfit, Blaze, followed close behind. **Not another bloody American invention.** 'Fraid so. Its style has since been appropriated by producers elsewhere, particularly in Italy where garage is still one of the prevalent sounds in today's clubs and the south-east of England where soul boys gradually caught on to this new sound. **Is this speed garage malarkey anything to do with garage then?** Although principally London-oriented, its roots are undoubtedly in America with producers such as Armand Van Helden, Todd Edwards and Masters At Work highly influential. Journalists love it, because it's a new genre of music they can write inaccurate articles about. Garage purists (of which there are a disturbing number cluttering up psychiatric wards the country over) hate it with a passion. **Most likely to ask...** "Is this love that I'm feeling?" **Least likely to ask...** "Does your chewing gum lose its flavour on the bedpost overnight?" **Not to be confused with...** House, bungalow, shed, out-house, weekend cottage in the Welsh hills.

I was interviewing Naomi Campbell who never gets off the phone. While she was having her hair done we could all hear her conversation and quickly figured she was chatting to one of her famous ex-boyfriends (an Italian-American actor type) who was filming in London and wanted to know which clubs to go to. **Naomi asked us what we thought, expecting us to direct him to some swank high-society A-list place.** We thought for a while and then sent Robert De Niro to Thunderdrive at Subterania and the Saturday Social at Turnmills. Beverley Holmes, journalist

It was back in 1992, one of my mates got hold of some really good Ecstasy so we went to the Arena in Middlesbrough where Dave Seaman was DJing. The pills were of the highest quality and by midnight we were really off it. A proper northern club night scream up. **Because the club finished at 2 am, people used to drive to this park a few miles out of town — maybe twenty or thirty cars — and we joined the convoy.** I got talking to some girl who gave me a rather good blow job while her boyfriend was sharing a spliff with my mates, blissfully unaware of the goings on fifty yards away in his girl's car. Nice one, matey. Chris Douglas, plasterer

Hip Hop

Born... The Bronx NYC, c. 1975. **With or without a hyphen?** There is still some debate about that. **To the hip hip hop and a hippety-hop and you, erm, don't stop?** Exactly, you seem to know, ahem, 'what time it is'. **Sure, but what's the difference between hip hop and rap?** Worldwide commercial success. **No, really.** Well, purists would argue (and they do) that rap is just a way of delivering lyrics, whereas hip hop is an entire culture. Hence, Ace Of Bass or The Outhere Brothers can be rap but certainly not hip hop. **Where can I find this culture?** In da ghetto of course. Try places like Brooklyn, Harlem ('Uptown'), South Central LA — anywhere with more sneaker stores than banks. **What does it look like?** It's quite scruffy, but often in a smart way **How will I recognise it?** Hip hop culture includes the holy trinity of rap music, graffiti and breakdancing, although most of the people who could ever breakdance have now got severely arthritic knees. **Could one rap about somewhere like Ipswich?** Probably not. Perhaps Ilford. **I've noticed baggy clothes. Do they play a part?** Indeed. The basic image is to look like you're in prison, but an expensive designer prison with plenty of logos. **And remedial spelling?** Not so prevalent these days, but still a safe bet. Try 'Bichasniguz' or 'Atak Of Da Bal-hedz' by Onyx. **I feel more hip hop already.** Steady. **What's it for exactly?** Elevating the iconography and rhetoric of the poor urban Black experience while introducing a contradictory tension by celebrating the worst excesses of American consumerist society. **You mean 'keepin' it real'.** Apparently. As long as keeping it real doesn't stop me owning several houses, fast cars and expensive suits and hanging out with people like Madonna and Sting. **What's the easiest way to become a hip hop legend?** Make some albums with titles like 'Kill Me Now', and 'I'm Hard And I Want To Die' and videos where you foretell your own brutal demise. Brag about how tough you are and how everyone else is a pussy unless they kill you (even if you're really an overfed mummy's boy, you have big eyelashes, used to write girly poetry and went to acting school). **Then what?** Just as you start hanging out with Madonna and Sting, someone takes your lyrics seriously and shoots you. **That's a bit harsh.** Listen, we don't want to encourage young kids to live violently, we just want to show the reality of what it's like to be poor and black in America. **Except for the bit about the showbiz parties.** Yes. **And the money?** OK. **And Sting and Madonna?** You got me there. **Who's Tim Westwood?** The son of a bishop from a village near Brighton. **What about trip hop?** That's just hip hop made by white people. **Not to be confused with...** Brit-pop, Top Shop, hopscotch. **Most likely to say...** Strictly 4 my niggaz. Wassup. Ya mama's so fat, when she put on heels she struck oil. **Least likely to say...** It's only entertainment.

I reckon there is only one great debate in the club fashion department. Sunglasses after dark: cool and dangerous or just plain dodgy? I used to be a paid-up member of the Shades Party but I eventually decided against them after visiting Tongue Kung Fu. The boys at TKF were in the habit of decorating whichever gaff they'd taken over with clothes on washing lines. That night, shades in place, I noticed a girl with an amazingly relaxed and rhythmic dancing style. A bright white light was shining from behind her and it made her look like a kind of angel. Well, I spent a while dancing near this vision of loveliness, and she faced me throughout. I smiled a big come-and-get-me-you-cheeky-minx smile, but I couldn't see her face clearly because of the light behind her. I plucked up the courage to say something and it was loud, so I moved as close to her ear as possible, only to find she didn't have an ear. She didn't have a head for that matter, either. I took the shades off and finally realised that I'd been leching over a tight-fit nylon sweater which had been hanging in the doorway. Shades are for sunshine, make no mistake' Michael Robinson, civil servant

Trainspotters

Born... They're not born. They're genetically created from mutant human waste. They're the Frankenstein's Monsters of the music industry. They're freaks. They're unnatural. **Steady on, you'll give yourself a hernia.** Well, I'm a bit annoyed at the moment. Someone called me a trainspotter yesterday. **Ahh, so you're a freak. A Frankenstein's Monster. A...** That's just it: they are. I'm not. Honestly! I'm normal, really I am. **But isn't that what they all say?** Yes, but I am. **So why did they call you a spotter then?** Someone asked me what Strictly Rhythm was. When I'd named the first forty-five releases and given him their address and phone number and recommended five or six of their best records and told him of all the great producers who had started their careers at Strictly, well, it was about then that he suggested that I was a spotter. **Sounds reasonable to me. Anyway, what is a trainspotter then?** It's someone who has an obsessive interest in a particular subject, be it trainspotting, or collecting autographs or, in this case, dance music. **These seem like perfectly normal hobbies for young chaps to get up to, after all it doesn't make you go blind.** They are normal up to a point and when that point is passed, well, then they become trainspotters and the fact that I wear strong-lensed glasses has nothing to do with my love for dance music. **It's hardly an illness though is it?** That's where you're wrong. In studies conducted in the US, doctors are claiming that this obsessive behaviour is, in fact, a mild form of autism. **Which is?** According to the dictionary definition, autism is, "an illness of the mind, especially in children, in which the imagination becomes too important and good relationships cannot be formed". **Ahem. Sounds a bit like you.** I've got loads of friends. You and... my parents. Actually my dad's stopped talking to me, so you and my mum. **And you think I'm a friend?** Anyway. Back to Stricty Rhythm. I don't know if you know, but their 100th single was in fact... **Least likely to say...** "I couldn't give a shit what the DJ's playing." **Most likely to say...** "It's funny you should mention that, because it reminds me of the 33rd release on Nu Groove, which I bought from Vinyl Mania in New York on a record shopping trip to America." **Not to be confused with...** Anything remotely normal.

1. Which football teams do the following DJs support?
a) Pete Tong
b) Little Louie Vega
c) Claudio Coccoluto
d) Paul Oakenfold

2. The eighties saw a boom in soul bands insisting on having a 'K' at the beginning of their name. Which one of the following is not a real band?
a) Kleavage
b) Krystol
c) Klique
d) Kleeer

3. Ce Ce Peniston sang with which band?
a) Tubby Terrier
b) Hungry Heifer
c) Overweight Pooch
d) Rotund Rottweiler

4. What is Frankie Knuckles' real name?
a) Francis Knockers
b) Francis Nicholls
c) Francis Knickers
d) Francis Knuckles

5. Billie Ray Martin formerly sang with which band?
a) Electribe 101
b) Shed Seven
c) Heaven 17
d) Haircut 100

6. Match the following DJs to the clubs they are associated with:
a) Mike Pickering   1) Sound Factory
b) Junior Vasquez   2) The Omen
c) LTJ Bukem   3) Haçienda
d) Sven Väth   4) Speed

7. What was the first record ever to be played on a Saturday night at the Ministry of Sound?
a) Elton John 'Saturday Night's Alright For Fighting'
b) Earth, Wind & Fire 'Saturday Nite'
c) T Connection 'Saturday Night'
d) De La Soul 'Saturdays'

8. Techno was first created in which city?
a) Chicago
b) Detroit
c) Barnsley
d) Philadelphia

9. Which DJ used the nom de plume Audrey Witherspoon whilst writing for a music magazine?
a) Andy Weatherall
b) Terry Farley
c) Pete Heller
d) Phil Perry

10. What is the correct name of the legendary vibes player/orchestra leader who played on Masters At Work's Nu Yorican Soul project?
a) Vince Arkansas
b) Vince California
c) Vince Indiana
d) Vince Montana

11. Producer/DJ/club legend Kris Needs was formerly the lead singer in which punk rock band?
a) Vice Squad
b) Vice Creams
c) Kreem Krackers
d) Ice T

12. Match the real christian name to the following club people:
a) Charlie Chester   1) Leroy
b) Norman Cook   2) Alexander
c) Sasha   3) Anthony
d) DJ SS   4) Quintin

13. Paul Shurey of Tribal Gathering fame was formerly the lead singer in which crap psychedelic band?
a) Mood Six
b) Moody Blues
c) Bar Six
d) Moodswings

14. Who were formerly known as the D.S. Building Contractors?
a) Chemical Brothers
b) Orbital
c) The Orb
d) Bentley Rhythm Ace

15. Which artist had a piece of work displayed on the wall leading to the bathrooms at the Ministry of Sound when it originally opened?
a) Damien Hirst
b) Rachel Whiteread
c) Goldie
d) Salvador Dali

16. What's Homer Simpson's favourite record?
a) Funkadelic 'One Nation Under A Groove'
b) Lipps Inc. 'Funkytown'
c) Baccara 'Yes Sir, I Can Boogie'
d) Abba 'Dancing Queen'

Answers on page 127

Voguing

Strike a pose! Fierce! **Not that gay arm-waving nonsense?** That's the one. **I saw this queen at Pushca doing it. Looked really stupid.** A pale imitation of the true art. It doesn't travel well. **So where can I see the real thing?** Ask a pier queen to show you his balls. **Come again?** Love to. Pier queens are the mostly black gay kids who hang out on the downtown piers in Manhattan. Balls are their parodies of glamorous fashion shows, held in musty church halls. It all started in Harlem in the sixties you know. Try and see Jenny Livingstone's Paris Is Burning. **Of course.** They're organised into 'houses', sort of gay street-gangs with names like Milan, Armani, Revlon, Ashanti, Africa, and Elite. Each with a 'mother', a 'father' and their 'children'. **Can I start my own, House Of Commons, House Of Fraser?** Check the name isn't taken. There's already the International House Of Pancakes, and a House Of Goddammit... **Then what?** Then you would 'walk', do 'battle' and 'throw shade' on your opponent, who might use some bitchy comments to try and 'read' you. If the 'category' requires it, you will also be going for 'realness' (eg passing as a real woman). Win, and you'll be displaying 'overness' — a total state of being. Perfection. **Which categories would I be good at?** Each ball dreams up its own. There are always regulars like 'Face' and 'Body', but try: 'Runway Punishment — There's A Score To Be Settled And Only Those Walking Bitches Will Survive' or 'Big Bad Girls Vs The Small Call Girl Vs The Amazon Hooker' or 'Costume — Cher vs Grace Jones'. For '9–5, White Collar Only' you should appear as a rigidly straight businessman. For 'Drug-Dealer Realness' quilted jackets, cellphones and briefcases full of white powder would be the order of the day. **Can't I enter them all?** Each specifies what particular brand of gender-bender can enter. Contestants are either 'Gentlemen' (straight-acting gay men), or 'Ladies' (transexuals and transvestites). Very occasionally you might see 'Ladies of Distinction' (born and bred women) or 'Ladies of Special Preference' (lesbians). **You haven't mentioned voguing, what's all that waving?** 'Performance' is the favoured term. Forget Madonna's poncy slow-motion stuff. It should be a millimetre-accurate flurrying of limbs with plenty of raunchy gymnastics. Show that you're dripping with glamour and your opponent's a dowdy uncoordinated loser. **It's a 'battle', you say?** Like rapping but with more make-up. **And Madonna started it all?** "I'm looking for what Madonna didn't have, and what she wished she had, and what she might have if she keeps watching" — an MC encouraging contestants at a Brooklyn ball at the height of Madonna's 'Vogue'. Erm, no. (though two of her dancers José and Luis came from Xtravaganza, the Sound Factory's house. They had a big flop on Mad's label with 'The Queens English') **What about Malcolm McClaren?** He too, tried to appropriate it, but the world wasn't ready for an ageing ginger punk striking a pose. **Can girls do it?** Only June of the House Of Nubia. **Not to be confused with...** Gurning, bogling, step aerobics, guiding aeroplanes. **Most likely to say...** Ovah! Worrrrrk! Fie-erce! **Least likely to say...** I must give you the name of my gynacologist.

Design Classics

Naked midriffs pulling the eye dangerously downwards, pert podium asses swishing out from snatch-hugging miniskirts, soft breasts breaking through wisps of stringy, furry, touch-me fabric: male clubbers can rejoice in the fact that a decade of dancing has done more for the female figure than even the most intensive of aerobics courses could have achieved.

But there's a flaw in the design: try and get a conversation going with one of these disco-vixens, or even just offer them a smile, and you'll find out fast that their sexual promise is about as sincere as a footballer's marriage vows. Sure they got dressed with a seventies issue of Playboy for style guidance, and if they were at the beach they'd be butt-bare enough to avoid a tan-line, but flirt and look happy? They'd sooner get dressed and go home.

Hey, we were born to suffer. Us real men ride roughshod over the frustration of a roomful of prick-teasing ball-breakers and their 'get-a-hard-on-but-don't-chat-me-up' sleaze and tease. Instead we concentrate on the real girls in the party — the girls, nay women, who know there's a point to looking club-sexy beyond getting in Mixmag or pissing off your fat friend Paula, and that point is to HAVE SOME FUN.

Remember ladies, porno-minded flyer designers have fought long and hard for your right to stand in front of a speaker wearing a fluffy bra and silver knickers, don't let them down.

060

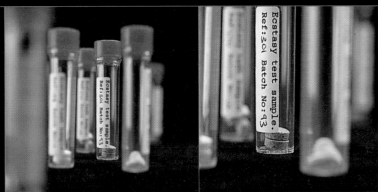

If anything is an object of desire it's an Ecstasy tablet.

3, 4-methylenedioxymethylamphetamine, MDMA, Adam, E, XTC, X, a chemical compound which changed the world. Just add music and a crowd and you have the perfect formula for a peak experience. It's a pharmaceutical reset button for years of being someone else. Strip back the falseness of trying to be a contender, take a pill and be yourself.

From 1985 when London trendies brought back New York MDMA made for mystic psychotherapy by Texan hippies, to the present day when mad schemies in Edinburgh sweat in dark hardcore-hangars necking multiple pills smuggled in by Scally gangsters from factories in the former Soviet union, Ecstasy has played a central role in revolutionising our culture. It's been illegal since 1977 (1985 in the US), and it goes through periods where it's dangerously unreliable or decidedly uncool, but out of people who've tried it once, only 11% have never done it again.*

Ecstasy is such a successful design, with such a widespread marketing network (chances are you buy it from a friend rather than a faceless dealer) that it has put one of the world's most established industries (brewing) and one of the world's oldest products (alcohol) on the defensive. If you can get a £10 buzz that lasts several hours, why spend £2 a pint getting blotto.

It was first synthesised as a diet pill in 1912 by a German pharmaceutical company, and forgotten until the mid-sixties when Californian Alexander Shulgin cooked it up again and spread it around academic psychotherapy circles. The New York gay scene was where it first met dance music.

It arrived in London courtesy of international party animals like Mark Almond and Boy George, and was then introduced to UK club culture on a mass scale from the wild parties of Ibiza.

Scare stories, tabloid outrage and the occasional well-publicised Ecstasy tragedy can't overpower the personal experiences of a whole generation of young people, and statistically it's a safe drug (around 100 documented deaths in a decade compared to alcohol's annual five-figure death toll). However, don't forget we're all living a huge experiment. Although medical studies are being done and seasoned users examined, there is no medical understanding of the drug's long-term effects. The wild tales about Parkinson's disease, drained spinal fluid, kidney problems, lasting loss of serotonin and brain damage may still turn out to be true. Besides, the medium term psychological effects are already well known: do too many Es too often and those woeful Wednesdays start blending together into one long depression.

Like the buzz, it's been fun while it lasted: thousands of strangers dancing in unity, football thugs hugging on the terraces, life-changing music made in Essex bedrooms, entrepreneurs turning mad schemes into real businesses. Doves, apples, white burgers, snowballs, rhubarb and custards, half moons, they changed the world. But go easy: the last pill I saw had a skull and crossbones on one side and "Killer" on the other.

* from MTV/European Commission 1997, the largest ever survey into European youth attitudes.

The Urei Mixer

Mobile Phones

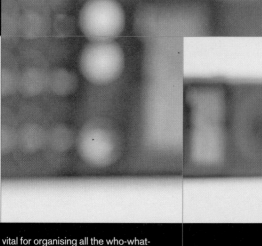

Most of you won't even know what a Urei mixer is. Still less of you will care. But, let us tell you, the Urei mixer is a thing of great beauty and, sadly, a thing of the past. The Urei 1620 is so simple and yet so quintessentially perfect that to use one once is to be addicted. The Urei 1620 — and its predecessor, the equally wonderful Bozak — is a poke in the eye to modern technology without a micro-chip or digital-delay system in sight. It built its reputation on the east coast of the United States as the mixer for the discerning club jock during the seventies and its quality is such that today you will still find most New York clubs have them. Fitted with simple 'pots' (knobs rather than sliders for smooth mixing) to handle one is to understand the tactile beauty of a DJ's job. The extra outputs it's fitted with also make it perfect for modern aural requirements: reel-to-reels, DAT machines, CD players and extra decks. The Urei is no longer manufactured, but you can generally buy them for around £1,500. If you can find one.

"Look at the width on that. Nasty." Nowadays we've all got one, so it's easy to forget the image that went with owning one of the first generation of mobile phones. As you power-lifted that 2lb slab of Apollo 13-era electronics to your ear, and nuked several thousand brain cells with its wayward microwave transmissions, you could almost hear the whispers: "Must be a dealer."
The mobile phone hit our shores the same year as house music. It allowed pirate radio to flourish, letting DJs receive calls from their listeners, whatever condemned tower block they were currently clinging to, and its popularity grew massively because it was the perfect communication tool for co-ordinating raves. Organisers used BT's new 0898 premium rate pre-recorded phone lines to announce the location, changing the announcement as the final details got closer and closer, and thousands of punters circled mudfields in the home counties, calling in on their mobiles to find out the party was moved/raided/a scam/happened last week. A mobile is the essential club accessory,

vital for organising all the who-what-wheres of a night out. Soon we'll all be like the Italians with super slimline Ericssons and Motorolas, set on vibrate so we can feel them ringing on the dancefloor. Mobile phones have been used to detonate bombs, to avert air hijacks, and to reveal royal tampon fantasies to the world. Use them too much and you could risk Alzheimer's disease, asthma or cancer, say scientists. At least back in the M25 days the battery wore out quickly enough to let the drugs fry your brain before your phone did.

Nicky Holloway All-Night Petrol Stations Rizla

If he hadn't existed we would have had to have invented him. There's something a little bit cheesey, a little bit sleazy and, well, a little bit perfect about Nicky Holloway. Something about the way he's earned fortunes and lost them; or left the house wearing clothes and returned home without them. And the clubs he's organised: the soul nights at the Swan & Sugar Loaf in Bermondsey; the Special Branch parties in London Zoo and the Natural History Museum; discovering Ibiza and those subsequent acid house nights at Sin and The Trip; KAOS Weekenders; the Milk Bar and the Velvet Underground.

Two stories. An acolyte of Nicky's went upstairs to get paid at the Trip: "We went into this little office at the Astoria, opened the door and looked around. There was just money everywhere, on the sofas, on the desk, on the floor. I'd never seen so much money in my life." Then there's the gig in Helsinki when he turned the volume down in the middle of his set and shouted: "Can someone please bring me some drugs!" Nicky Holloway is all about money and madness and drugs and fun and sleaze. And he's got quite good taste in music.

With all honesty, who can say that they have never uttered the immortal mantra: "Ten Silk Cut, a packet of king-size Rizlas, a carton of Ribena and a pint of milk, please."? Throw in the occasional pack of tea bags, thin white sliced loaf of Sunblest and — if you're really caned — an indescribable pink fluffy toy with a stomach that squeaks when you squeeze it and you have the makings of a perfectly messy Sunday morning party. Thanks to the peculiarly archaic way in which British commerce operates, the petrol station holds a unique place in the affections of its youth. Like its forebear, the motorway service station (the north-west section of the M6 and M3's Fleet services being particular favourites), the petrol station holds this particular position by virtue of one thing alone: it happens to be the only thing open at four o'clock on a very cold morning in November.

Okay, so in design classic terms, they're never going to vie with a Richard Rogers building or Terence Conran restaurant and frankly, they're all the better for it. They stink of petrol, have bars on the windows and treat you like criminals. Could they be any more perfect?

If anyone knows of anything more perfectly designed for the consumption of narcotics than a pack of king size Rizlas, then we've yet to hear about it.

Okay, so some prefer to go about the job the long way, welding three regular Rizla papers to make one giant one. Heck, some people even prefer to smoke a hefty wodge of Samson shag in them (perish the thought). We'll conveniently overlook the Rizla company's in-denial attitude towards their perfect product (King size is for smoking BIG cigarettes? Yeah, right).

If further proof is required of the perfection of Rizla, a hop over to Europe or America should suffice. Papers are strange shapes (who ever devised a square paper; and for what nefarious purpose?), with so little glue on the edge that less than a minute after creating your latest work of considerable art, you're left holding a crumpled riot of white and brown mush. No, you can keep your foreign papers and your fancy continental ways where rolling papers are concerned. Paper that holds firm and true while the job's being done. Glue that sticks first time. And a shape surely sent down from heaven (or, at the very least, Morocco). There is only one rolling paper. It's called Rizla.

There's Purdeys, Aqua Libra, Red Bull and eighty-eight flavours of Ribena. And then there's the original: that strange boiled-sweet colour, that loose glucose flavour (it's made from real sugar you know), the first bottle to have that gulpy spout — Lucozade. There are obvious reasons why Lucozade became the drink of the summer of love. It gives you the dancefloor NRG you need, it doesn't dull the MDMA like beer. But Shoomer Steve Proctor argues that it was just in the right place at the right time. "Lucozade became the drink for no other reason than because it was the thing they sold at The Fitness Centre — if they only sold Milk Stout it would have been that." Lucozade sued rave pop star Adamski when he made the connection and put it on a record sleeve, but their marketing men quickly flipped the scenario and used the track for a TV ad. And? "It's Isotonic." Thanks Barnesy.

Ask a DJ which record decks he uses and as sure as night follows day, and headache follows lager-frenzy, he will say: "Technics". Never mind model numbers, everyone knows what he's referring to: the Technics 1200 and its slinky younger black brother, the 1210. Go to a club — any club in the world — and there will be a minimum of two 1200s. They are now industry standard, uniting behind their banner every faction of the dance world from hip hop kids' turntable devilry, to house DJs' smooth blending. Everyone uses them, everyone swears by them.
Following on from the SP-15 and SP-1500 (which many DJs who actually used them preferred to the 1200), the original 1200, the Mark 1, was introduced in 1973, after being developed by Shuuichi Obata, Seiichi Ushijma, and Haryuki Otani at parent company Panasonic. It had a direct drive system, meaning that unlike the more common belt drives, the platter was welded directly to the motor. The vari-speed on the Mark 1 was a two-button affair at the front of the deck with an LED screen which went up (or down) in 0.5%

gradients (though no-one is certain as to why the vari-speed was there — it was widely believed to be for karaoke).
In November 1980, Technics introduced an updated version, the Mark 2, which added the now familiar vari-speed slider to the right of the turntable. It hasn't changed since (save for the introduction of the 1210 Mark 2 in April 1986). But then, it hasn't needed to. Whilst the rest of the industry has come up with cheaper — and vastly inferior — versions, no-one has yet come up with a product to rival the simplicity and longevity of the 1200. Dance music now has its equivalent of rock's Fender Stratocaster.

Smiley

The 303

The icon of acid house. Smiles, happiness, love, joy: a pill-round face with a dumb-eyed grin. "Have a nice day!" In the early-seventies it was a badge pinned onto gentle, acid-traumatised hippies (or a churched-up lefty's CND rucksack). Talking Heads put it on their sleeve for 'Psycho Killer', suggesting that such nice happy people might be a little unbalanced, then Alan Moore upped the irony factor even more by splashing blood on smiley's pretty yellow grin in his 1987 graphic novel The Watchmen, followed by Bomb The Bass's sleeve for 'Beat Dis'. From here it was a speedy journey to underground drug culture. Danny Rampling sprinkled smileys on his Shoom flyers like a shower of pills (he claims the idea came from a smiley-badged stylist called Barnaby), the Shoomers made themselves smiley t-shirts, and it was soon the official enduring symbol for acid house and 1988's Summer of Love. Smiley even became a regular tabloid cover star (they flipped his grin into a disapproving scowl when they figured out the drug connection) and appeared on market-stall t-shirts across the land. If you believe Hollywood, he was invented by fictional fuckwit Forrest Gump.

Long before Hardfloor and Josh Wink turned it into a laughable substitute for rock-masturbation — the guitar solo of the nineties, if you will — the Roland TR-303 Bassline was firstly an abject commercial failure, then the freakiest instrument ever to be committed to badly-pressed crackly vinyl. Created as to go with the TR-606 drum machine, it was originally designed for guitarists to play along to (oh, irony of ironies!). Unfortunately, it was so difficult to programme that only boffins with degrees in quantum physics had any hope of making it work. Having been launched in 1982 (at a retail price of £215), Roland ceased manufacture a mere eighteen months later.

Its saving grace was the set of filters provided for no discernible reason whatsoever which, when twiddled and panned, created a strange 'acid' sound. This sound initially found its way on to a record by Phuture called 'Acid Trax', by a trio of teenagers from Chicago, Herb Jackson, Nathaniel Jones (aka DJ Pierre) and Spanky. The 'acid' in the record was not a reference to drugs, as Spanky says, "It was never our intention for it to be linked

to drugs. We thought of 'acid rock' which had the same change in frequencies." This, of course, didn't stop thousands of kids in the UK getting 'on-one, matey' to the sound of 'Acid Trax', however. Thanks to the 303, house had 'acid' prefacing it and the Sun had found a new menace to replace the miners.

As a result of its success (having been able to pick one up for £50 in a junk shop a few years back, you'd be lucky to find one under £1,000 nowadays), Roland introduced the MC-303 Groove Box in 1997, showing that you just can't keep a good invention down, no matter how old-fashioned it may seem. As 'Mad' Mike Banks of Detroit techno terrorists once put it, "The wheel is the type of invention that trendy people might say is old, but every time that fucking aeroplane lands, your ass is riding on wheels. Like the wheel, the 303 is a perfect invention."

The Places

If one club could be said to have created the blueprint for the modern-day discotheque it is the Loft. Clubs like Arthur, run by Richard Burton's second wife, Suzy, in the mid-sixties, could claim to have shaped what a modern New York disco would look like. Other clubs could claim they shaped how it would sound — there were already DJs who had begun to forsake talking between records in order to create a seamless ebb and flow of music, for instance Francis Grasso of the Sanctuary on 43rd Street. But none of these clubs combined all of the elements quite like the Loft. It was neither a sassy backdrop for the jet-set to sip cocktails to, nor was it a steamy gay club with sex as the main course on the menu. The Loft was personality driven. It was the culmination of all of the beliefs of the man that created it (and, who, to this day, is still running it): David Mancuso.

Mancuso is a raggedy-looking guy, with a beard that made him look like a roadie for the Grateful Dead. He became the host, the promoter and the DJ.

The original site of the Loft was an old factory on Broadway near Bleecker Street, in the downtown area of Manhattan. It wasn't a plush space fitted with the latest lights. In fact, it was where Mancuso lived. It was a rambling loft with various rooms divided up for working and living spaces. All told, though, it held more than enough people to make a great party.

The idea was simple. The guests (originally just acquaintances of Mancuso) would be invited, and each guest would be given a card which would allow them to bring their friends along. And then they would be given cards, and so on. Before long thousands of people from all over the five boroughs of New York (and sometimes well beyond) had these cards. Entrance was a four or five dollar tax. No alcohol was served, but juice and fruit was freely available. But the reason people came to the Loft was the music and the quality of the sound system which Mancuso had put together: Paul Klipsch speaker system, Mark Levinson amplifiers, Mitchell Cotter turntable bases and line amplifier and hand-crafted cartridges by Koetsu.

Mancuso's style was not really that of a modern DJ, though the end result was. Latterly, Mancuso didn't even use a mixer, preferring instead to simply cue one record to the next, relying on the quality of the records he played to whip the floor into a tornado of sexual energy. He was never afraid to drop the tempo if the mood suited. Larry Levan, later the resident at the Paradise Garage, was heavily influenced by David Mancuso, as were most of the subsequent generation of New York jocks, from Madonna collaborator Shep Pettibone to Frankie Knuckles. As Levan put it, "I used to watch people cry in the Loft for a slow song because it was so pretty."

Many of the early disco staples became bona fide classics in the Loft: MFSB's 'Love Is The Message', perhaps the first disco record, as well as a bewilderingly eclectic array of records by bands such as Barrabas (a Spanish funky rock act discovered by Mancuso on a trip to Spain) and Wood, Brass & Steel, whose 'Funakanova' many of today's clubbers would recognise after Black Science Orchestra sampled it heavily on 'New Jersey Deep'. "That place changed my world around 360 degrees, musically," recalls producer David Morales. "He had the greatest sound system. There were balloons all over the ceiling, no fancy lighting. Primitive. Sometimes they would even have acid punch."

The Loft later transplanted a few hundred yards to 99 Prince Street in SoHo and has been re-born several times since. Emerging in the late-eighties as Choice in the East Village, after promoter-cum-DJ Richard Vasquez helped Mancuso relaunch it, it has moved at least twice since with sporadic parties still being held even today. Even though Mancuso now seems like a man slightly out of his time, he — along with Levan — was the most influential American DJ and his club one of its great archetypes.

If one club could be said to have created the blueprint for the modern-day discotheque it is the Loft

Never has a club had so many column inches devoted to it as Studio 54. It was the superclub before the term was ever dreamt of. It was a club of its time: drugs, sex and cult of the celebrity — late-seventies New York in essence. The music was almost incidental and few people ever knew who the DJ was (he was called Richie Kaczor). Look at the pictures and they tell not a story of dancing, but of trashed celebrities half hanging off the banquettes that provided relief from the Bacchanalian excesses going on elsewhere. Look! There's Elton John sat next to Andy Warhol; and who's that talking to Andy? Why, it's Jerry Hall. And that guy over there with Mick Jagger? Oh, Mikhail Baryshnikov. Great clubs are forged out of a happy coincidence of events. Simply being there at the right time (as the Haçienda discovered with acid house) can mark a club out as extraordinary. In reality Studio 54 was not a great club in the same sense as most of the clubs written about in this book, but in many ways it represents the New York of our fervid imaginations more than the Paradise Garage. The fact that much of it is based on what little facts are known about it, is neither here nor there; we'd rather skim over the realities and live the dream, like most creatures of the night. And it's a dream that ended in disaster for its two protagonists.

Studio 54 rose on 254 West 54th St. in Manhattan on April 26th 1977, a product of the excited minds of a pair of relative greenhorns in the nightworld business, Ian Schrager and Steve Rubell. Schrager, the straight man (in both senses of the word) happy in the background, and Rubell, a gay man with a prodigious propensity for drug-taking and partying, were the perfect partnership and their flair for publicity and drama made Studio an almost instantaneous hit.

The opening night was so overcrowded with the typical mélange of celebrity, club kids and the Big Apple's demi-monde, that many were locked out, as Cher and Margaux Hemingway danced into the headlines of the New York tabloids simply by virtue of being there. A couple of nights later, a hastily organised birthday party for Bianca Jagger sealed the club's reputation as she arrived on a white horse, surrounded by two women adorned only in gold body paint. The pictures were wired around the world. Studio 54 was nothing if not a great photo opportunity.

The club's door policy was legendary. It was easier to get into Albania than Studio 54. One of the doormen, Baird Jones, recalls an occasion that demonstrated just how desperate people were to get it in. "There was this girl that wanted to come in the club. She was a ravishingly beautiful girl, okay? Steve told me to tell her that if she took all her clothes off she could get into the club for free. She took all her clothes off… And she had to go to the hospital with frostbitten nipples!" A club associate, Al Corley, said of the door policy: "You know Steve's basic line? 'Just make sure you don't let anyone in like me!'" It was a joke, but there was some truth in it. Neither Schrager nor Rubell would have got into their own club. (Later, Chic's Nile Rogers and Bernard Edwards would be refused entry. In protest, they went home and recorded a song called 'Fuck Off'. It was later changed to 'Le Freak' and became one of the biggest selling dance records of all time.)

The stories of sexual antics were legion. Reveller Richard Turley remembers an incident outside the club: "I got there a little late and there were over a thousand people outside. We were three or four layers back

and there were thirty or forty layers behind us. This doctor started handing Quaaludes [seventies US version of Valium] out. They took about fifteen or twenty minutes to kick in. About thirty people standing round us took them and then everybody started having this mad sexual orgy. All the men had their dicks out… the women were showing their tits… everybody was feeling everybody else". Inside it was the same story. Normally straight men snuck up to the balcony to receive blowjobs off transvestites; in the basement there was a small cubicle with wall-to-wall mattresses for those that could manage to get it together.

And then there was the famous Man in the Moon crescent-shaped logo, with a coke spoon that would arc towards its nose, releasing a sparkling array of lights upwards as if triggered by narcotics. Studio 54 resembled nothing so much as the last days of the Roman Empire. Disaster inevitably arrived on December 14th 1978 when the FBI raided the club after being tipped off about alleged 'skimming' (skimming is where a percentage of the cash at the door is skimmed off the top of the takings and not declared). They found an incriminating set of second books in the safe and, much worse, they found black plastic bag after black plastic bag stuffed full of dollars hidden in the ceiling of the club, $500,000 in all. As the raid was happening, a cocky Steve Rubell turned up at the club. A further $100,000 was discovered in the trunk of his car. Further raids to his home unearthed more bags concealed behind the bookshelf. A safe-deposit box at Citibank brought another haul of $900,000. The final tally was $2.5m. To compound their problems, a book that Schrager was carrying as the raid was in progress, concealed five bags of white powder (it later tested positively as cocaine). In true Studio style, they opened for business that night and the ensuing tabloid splashes ensured that they registered their biggest night ever at the club.

They finally appeared before US District Judge Richard Owen for sentencing on January 18th, 1980, where they received three and a half years for tax evasion. And, although they were released the following January, things would never be the same again. Of the pair Schrager was the one most obviously affected by his experiences of jail (his father Max, too, had wound up in prison). Studio 54 was reopened on September 15th, this time promoted by Jim Fouratt and Rudolf, who later became a key face in New York. It was rammed with the old faces: Halston, Andy Warhol, John Belushi, Jack Nicholson, Ryan O'Neal. It stayed open for a while, but was never really the same again.

The duo went on to buy a hotel, Morgan's, but, sadly, Rubell died of an AIDS-related illness on July 25th 1989. Subsequently, Schrager has become one of the most respected high-class hoteliers in America, with the Royalton in New York occupying pride of place in his empire. After several attempts to reopen it under different management (all were flops), the Studio held one final bash in July 1996 before it was demolished to make way for a virtual entertainment centre.

However, interest in the club seems to be gaining momentum. At the time of writing, a documentary, The Last Dance, had just been produced for US network TV and two movies — The Last Days Of Disco and 54 (the latter starring Mike Myers as Rubell) — are in production. There are also reports that the owners of London's Café De Paris intend to rennovate and reopen the club some time in 1998. Somehow, the memory of Studio 54 lives on.

03 Paradise Garage, New York

> "America is a very narrow-minded place, and these were people who shared something: an open mind. It wasn't just about getting high either"

"As you climb its steeply angled ramp to the second floor you feel like a character in a Kafka novel. From overhead comes the heavy pounding of the disco beat like a fearful migraine. When you reach the 'bar', a huge bare parking area, you are astonished to see immense pornographic murals of Greek and Trojan warriors locked in sado-masochistic combat running from floor to ceiling. On the floor of the main dancing room are the most frenzied dancers of the disco scene: the black and Puerto Rican gays, stripped down to singlets and denim shorts, swinging their bodies with wild abandon."
Albert Goldman, Disco

If the Paradise Garage had never existed, the Ministry of Sound would never have been built. To this day, the myth of the Garage continues apace, undoubtedly aided by the untimely death of its pivotal character and resident DJ, Larry Levan and equally the fact that a genre of music, garage, was named after the club.
The Paradise Garage on King Street in Manhattan, opened its doors in 1977 after Levan, Richard Long (the constructor of its sound system) and cohorts (including Mel Cheren of leading disco label, West End Records) finally raised sufficient cash to open a small room in the space they had leased. Like Levan's previous residencies it was an almost immediate success, thus began its ten year reign over New York clubland.
What set the Garage apart from the more media-friendly clubs of uptown Manhattan (such as Studio 54 and Xenon) was its relationship to its members. As Steven Harvey, author of the famous Collusion article on New York disco, said at the time, "When I first went to the Paradise Garage I felt as though I'd finally found the perfect nightclub. With a clear door policy — members and their guests only — a kind and courteous staff, no liquor, an awesome sound system continuously expounding the most serious black music and an audience of thousands of dancers whose inter-connected energy often makes the main dance room feel like a rocket at the point of lift-off. Here was the antidote to all the glacial pose palaces passing as dance clubs."

Keyboard player Michael DeBenedictus — who collaborated with Levan on his band project the Peech Boys and later played live at the Garage — recalled in an interview in the NME: "There's no other focus than the music. People come to dance and they take it seriously. The best dancers in the world are there. They don't come to cruise, they don't come to get drunk or get high. They come to dance. For fourteen hours. You see all the break dancing, electric boogie, all the stuff."
The Garage not only created such a space, but continued to recreate it year after year. Its members lived for it. "I saw Lace perform 'Can't Play Around' at the Garage," remembers DJ Danny Tenaglia. "And the record was so huge there that you almost couldn't hear any of the singing. That's how crazy the crowd were going. When they finished, we kept on screaming until they came out and sang it again. I probably stayed there for about fifteen minutes with chills and goosebumps all over me. It's those kind of memories that make me believe I'll never experience anything like it again."
Dave Piccioni, owner of Black Market Records in London, was a leading DJ in New York towards the end of the Garage's tenure: "It was the late-eighties when I was going. It was New York cut-throat money time. Everybody was sticking knives in each other's backs. It was dog eat dog; aggressive; drug-dealing was rife; there were 60,000 people living on the street. It was a dog of a place to live in. And then you'd go to this little oasis, where people were really well-mannered and friendly to each other. You just felt completely comfortable. America is a very narrow-minded place and these were people who shared something: an open mind. The thing they had in common wasn't just getting high, like it is here, it was much more than that. That was what was so great about it."
It was in this climate that a word to describe the music Levan played became the new dance industry buzzword: 'Garage music'. It's a word that has since become a hopeless corruption of Levan's style (although one of the many facets to his DJing was, indeed, the soulful New Jersey-style vocal tracks that are closely identified with garage). As Tony Humphries said, "You can't even define Garage music, because it was music that was played at the club at that time in that era; but we're talking about a ten year span. Records by The Rolling Stones ('Too Much Blood') and Talking Heads ('Once In A Lifetime') were played. If you played them now, people would say, 'that's not a Garage record'. But it was."
The Paradise Garage finally closed its doors in September 1987 and immediately left a void in New York. You still meet people in the city who couldn't bring themselves to go to another club, such was its impact. And even now, over ten years later, it is still an inspiration for clubs and DJs the world over.

04 Warehouse/Music Box, Chicago

PANIC BUTTON

DJ WORK LIGHT
DIMMER

DJ WORK LIGHT
POWER ON.OFF

074

The Warehouse: a three-storey factory building on a broad, sodium-lit street in west central Chicago, the club after which a whole genre of music will be named. It's the early eighties, Saturday after midnight, and a line of people — mostly gay, nearly all black, and all tense with excitement — waits on a stairway to enter by the top floor. They are dressed with elegance but in clothes ready for sweat. Most have just risen from sleep; many will be here until noon the next day. Once in the club, they head straight to the dark, sweaty dancefloor. They came here for Frankie Knuckles' music. They came to The Warehouse to dance.

"In the early days between 1977 and 1981 the parties were very intense," remembers Frankie. "It was amazing, because you had these down-to-earth, corn-fed mid-western folk, and yet the parties were very soulful, very spiritual. The scene we created at The Warehouse was something completely new to them, but once they latched onto it, it spread like wildfire throughout the city."

You reached the dancefloor at The Warehouse through a stairwell from the lounge above. Heat and steam drifted up to meet you, generated in the murk of the underlit room by the glistening black bodies that were down there 'jacking' away, their clothes reduced to a minimum of athletic gear. On occasion some even danced hanging from water pipes that ran across the room. Frankie would work the crowd, with mixes and edits: a New York phenomenon which Chicago clubs hadn't yet experienced. "Kids would totally lose their minds," remembers one regular. He played a soaring blend of underground disco, funk and soul, with hot new Philly tracks next to freaky Euro imports. It was not music we would describe as 'house', but it was where house would come from, the music and the vibe. Frankie still remembers the feeling of communion, the intense focus his club engendered. "For most of the people that went to The Warehouse, it was Church."

When he left in 1983 to found his own club, The Powerplant, his crowd followed him loyally, and the owners of The Warehouse pitched a new club against him: the Music Box, its resident a young DJ from California named Ron Hardy. Veteran Chicago producer Marshall Jefferson remembers being led to the Music Box by a girl he worked with who wore studded leather and pink hair. Intrigued, he told her, "I want to see the wild clubs you go to. She took me there and I was touched by God! The volume, man, just BOOM!!! It penetrated through my chest and took hold of my heart."

> "For most of the people that went to The Warehouse, it was Church"

Ron Hardy played with raw energy, completely in the moment. His music was about bombshells and surprises; repetitive edits and climax after funky climax. "It was Philadelphia stuff, black disco: moody, clubby stuff," recalls Jefferson. "Ron Hardy was the greatest DJ that ever lived."

"The first time I saw him spin it was his birthday," remembers seasoned clubber Cedric Neal, "and just to see people literally crying because this man had them so hyper, seeing people pass out. I was like 'Hey, this is my type of party.'" Cedric also recalls the sexual freedom that went with the place. He grins as he describes "the big speaker", ten feet tall, all the way at the back of the club, where couples would get under the stage. "We'd take girls in there: get a blowjob, a quickie. It was still the end of the sexual revolution." He remembers how there were pillows in the girls' bathroom "There'd be guys in there, getting high, having sex together."

The culture was taken from the gay core of original clubbers and there was no homophobia from the straight folk who swelled the growing scene. "If you couldn't stand to be around gays you didn't party in the city of Chicago," remembers Cedric. "They would ask 'Are you a child or a step-child?' meaning are you gay. If you were a step-child it meant you were straight but we accept you." It became fashionable for a time to act gay even if you weren't. He even recalls people who experimented with bisexuality as an attempt to get closer to the true meaning of house.

Club drugs like pot, poppers, (known as 'rush') and LSD were present, with a smattering of MDA, cocaine and Ecstasy. Music Box also had PCP or 'Angel Dust', a scary psychotic drug, in its veins. A popular high was 'happy sticks': joints dipped in PCP. With the resulting manic energy, the Music Box could be an intimidating place indeed. DJ Derrick Carter remembers being truly scared after sneaking in aged 17. "Ronnie would play something like Eddie Kendricks' 'Going Up In Smoke,' and everybody would be — going up in smoke! It would just lift everybody off the ground, people would be crying, and just freaking out, they got so charged."

The emotional intensity of clubs like Warehouse and Music Box, combined with the twin genius of Hardy and Knuckles gave Chicago a club scene that was truly unrivalled. And inspired by the godlike status their crowds awarded these star DJs, everybody suddenly wanted to play records and make music.

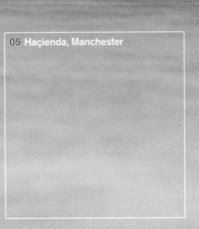

05 Haçienda, Manchester

"I'd been to New York and seen Danceteria and Paradise Garage. I just thought, why hasn't Manchester got one of those? Fucking New York's got one, we should have one."
Tony Wilson

It's the early eighties in Manchester and a reporter from London button-holes a pair of Mancunian goths as they emerge from one of the Haçienda's rival clubs. He asks them why they didn't go to the Haç. They reply: "Because they try and educate you with the music they play." No-one could have come closer to trying to explain what the Haçienda is and, moreover, what it represented than that simple, one-line damnation. Although the Haçienda will be remembered as the fulcrum around which 'Madchester' revolved, it was much more than that. It was a brave and largely successful experiment in punk-inspired Situationism; it was a haven from the violence and sullen stares of Manchester's less hospitable nightspots. The Haçienda single-handedly (and through sheer bloody-mindedness) gradually drew a whole city from its indie mentality towards the sound of raw black America and twisted British electronica.
Opened in 1982 by Factory Records honcho Tony Wilson, maverick popsters New Order and their manager Rob Gretton (who is credited with being its driving force) everything about the Haçienda was different. Its decor was a significant departure from the normal club. Designers Ben Kelly and Sandra Douglas had drawn on the graphic work of Peter Saville, whose sleeves for various post-punk acts had been highly influential. In Douglas's words they deliberately stayed away from, "some sort of disco extravaganza", opting instead for a quasi-industrial look that incorporated bollards on the edge of the dancefloor. Even before it opened, the Architectural Review described it as, "a significant milestone in British

The Haçienda drew a whole city from its indie mentality towards the sound of raw black America and twisted British electronica

interior design." Heck, it was even given a Factory Records catalogue number: Haç 51.

From the get-go, its musical policy followed the same revolutionary path, Bernard Manning was even the compère the night it opened. Initially more known as a live venue, it was not unusual to see Lloyd Cole follow Afrika Bambaataa; or Cabaret Voltaire precede Peech Boys. From its earliest days it had also had different club nights, with the odd funk or northern soul all-dayer thrown in. That said, it should be noted that its sound system was notoriously dreadful; it was only after New Order became more directly involved in the club did they go some way to rectify the problems with it.

The litany of nights is a lesson in popular British dance trends. There was Greg Edwards' Funk Night at which Run DMC performed, three years before their first UK hit. Chad Jackson's Big Noise provided the Saturday soundtrack in the mid-eighties. Jon Da Silva and Mike Pickering's cabaret extravaganza, Zumbar, had guests that ranged from Vera Duckworth to Dollar. One night, Nude, was hosted by a then unknown Graeme Park who'd defected from Nottingham's Garage in 1988. And then there was Wednesday's Hot, which led the north into acid house and swimming pools full of E'd up clubbers. Tony Wilson commented later, "Hot was great for us. Taking Pickering and Park's obscure house music and putting a swimming pool in the club was an excellent idea, so timely. It was at exactly the same moment as the balearic people dropped the balearic beats."

Haçienda's first public crisis occurred in July 1989 when a 16-year-old girl, Claire Leighton, died after buying a tablet of Ecstasy from someone in the club. It was the first big Ecstasy death story and one which gave then Manchester police chief James Anderton the opportunity to attack the club

— in April 1990 he declared his intention to oppose the renewal of the club's alcohol license. Even the Sun, no friend of the club scene, railed against Anderton in an editorial in July 1990, claiming that the Haç was the most important club in the north since the Cavern. Improbably, the Sun was right. It was an indisputable fact that university and polytechnic numbers had risen dramatically and, as James' Tim Booth said, "the Haçienda is Manchester's Eiffel Tower; a tourist attraction."

Amidst the mayhem, the club found time to organise a US tour (which encompassed Chicago, Miami, Boston, Detroit, LA and San Francisco) with current scions Dave Haslam, Mike Pickering, Graeme Park and Paul Oakenfold on DJing duty. But, as a result of mounting gang conflicts, the club itself took the decision to temporarily shut in 1991, despite winning its appeal for an alcohol license at the start of the year. The Haçienda reopened soon after, but gang warfare for control of the city's doors continued to mount, something which affected many more venues than just the Haçienda.

The Haçienda went into liquidation in 1997, and they were not the only ones. As house and dance music splintered hopelessly, many clubs in the city saw their natural constituencies diluted to the point of no return. The rumours continue as to whether the Haç will reopen though, in truth, it's almost irrelevant. The club that amongst others has launched the careers of Pickering, Park, Haslam, Laurent Garnier, Sasha and Justin Robertson has already staked an indisputable place in UK club history.

06 Taboo, London

'Strongly forbidden by social custom,' says the dictionary. In other words, Taboo was the antithesis of its name. That was the joke and the whole point. Taboo might just have been the first extended chapter in creator Leigh Bowery's career — he went on to design clothes for Boy George and pose for artist Lucian Freud — but it was also a seminal club in what it represented and went on to inspire. DJs Malcolm Duffy and Princess Julia started out as cloakroom attendants at Taboo. The DJs, Jeffrey Hinton, Mark Lawrence and Rachel Auburn, wore the trash aesthetic on their sleeves and in their record boxes. This was no Paradise Garage.

Until Taboo opened its doors at Maximus in Leicester Square in January 1985, London had been going through the thoroughly pretentious (and very straight) Hard Times look, supposedly a reflection of Thatcherism with 'Money's Too Tight To Mention' its trendy anthem. Bowery spat in the face of this convention, with outrageous glamour-wear and make-up so elaborate he made the members of Kiss look like Judith Chalmers. It was all about The Look; in fact it was easier to escape from Alcatraz than get into Taboo. Door-picker Mark Vaultier would hold up a mirror to Taboo-pretenders and ask: "Would you let yourself in?"

Once inside, of course, anything went (and frequently did). Ecstasy made its first clubland appearance at Taboo, with a precious few tablets filtering through to the chosen ones, bolstered by speed and alcohol. Sue Tilley, in her enthralling book on Leigh Bowery, recalls, "There were people snogging everywhere, girls and boys, girls and girls but mainly boys and boys. It was quite an education looking under the doors to see who was with whom and, because everyone knew everyone else, the news soon went flying round the club."

Everyone from Mick Jagger, Depeche Mode and Paul Weller to Patrick Cox and Bananarama were spotted at the club. But the centre of all the fun was Bowery and his sidekick Trojan, both frequently to be found legs akimbo on the dancefloor. Photographer and club columnist Dave Swindells remembers DJ Jeffrey Hinton rushing from the DJ booth one night and spinning around Bowery until they both fell to the floor laughing hysterically. Eighteen months later, like all good things, Taboo came to an end. But it set in train a series of clubs that have been inspired either directly or indirectly by it. Kinky Gerlinky, hosted by Michael and Gerlinde Kostiff, was a direct descendant of the glam days of Taboo. Originally housed at Legends, it switched to the Empire in Leicester Square in 1992 where it provided a focal point for London's clothes-horses. It was a place where men could come as women and women could come as whatever. Leigh Bowery once put on a legendary performance there, giving mock-birth to a baby (actually his long-suffering assistant Nicola) complete with fake blood and a string of sausages for an umbilical cord.

Whilst Geoff Oakes may well have been inspired by Shelley's to start his own club, Renaissance, his ideas were founded in clubs like Gerlinky and Taboo. The over-reaching mock-grandeur was a shock to the system — not least because it was in Mansfield, of all places — but it chimed perfectly with the times. The growth of the more dressy Balearic network of Venus, Most Excellent, Boys Own and Flying had also marked a turn away from the hippie sensibilities of the initial wave of acid house clubs. And whilst Renaissance became identified by the unique sound carved out by residents John Digweed and Sasha, it's the look and attitude that give it its stamp of clubbing authenticity. A look and attitude that Taboo pioneered.

> Bowery spat in the face of convention, with outrageous make-up so elaborate it made the members of Kiss look like Judith Chalmers

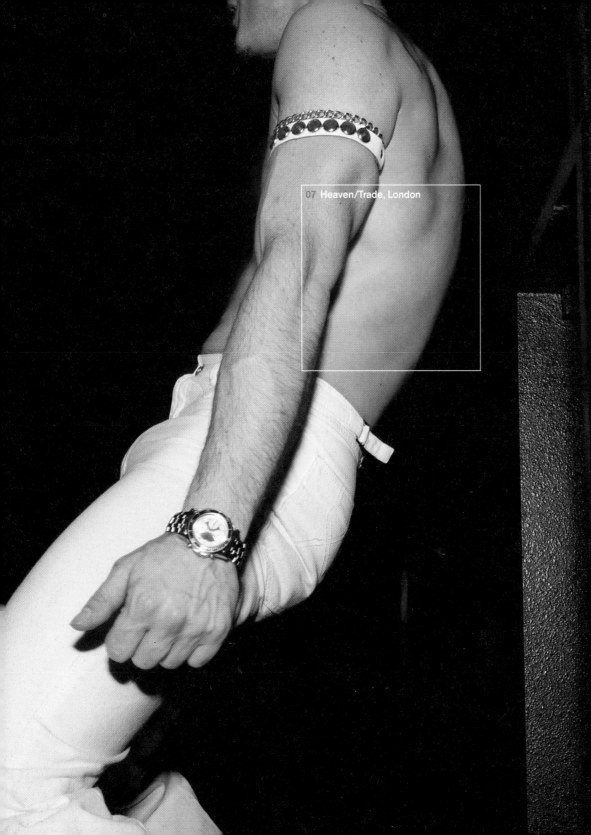

"The media in Italy has a really bad view of the discos. They are saying that they are factories to kill people." Gigi D'Agostino, Italian dream house DJ

On Dec 6th 1979, 2000 men were crammed into one of the railway arches underneath Charing Cross Station, listening to the bizarre twenties-style disco of Dr Buzzards Original Savannah Band played at a whisper. At the stroke of midnight, the club was pitched into darkness and an American actor called Doug Lambert biblically intoned the words above. Then, as the lights flashed the place into a celestial laserdrome and the crowd gasped with amazement, the storming sweeping pump of Dan Hartman's 'Relight My Fire', complete with Loleatta Holloway's screaming middle section, transformed the place into a mass of jumping male bodies. From that moment on, Heaven was on Earth.

Until Heaven opened its doors, gay London was a murky, secretive world. There were clubs to go to, but these were mostly private drinking dens with strict membership rules imposed on them by the authorities. Queer clubbing in the seventies usually meant cooling your heels outside an unmarked door in Soho waiting for someone to sign you in. So when entrepreneur Jeremy Norman took over a former rollerdisco called Global Village and fitted it out with a state of the art lights and sound system, insisted on a men-only door policy and opened it five nights a week, he was taking a big gamble.

His vision paid off and Heaven has been with us for nearly two decades, housing many grand and famous clubs, inspiring many others and securing its place in a great many legends. In addition to long being Europe's largest gay club, the place was the venue for Colin Faver's ground-breaking Asylum in 1981, the acid house crossover club Spectrum in 1987, and the hippie-trippy festival-in-a-bottle Megatripolis of 1994, while the Soundshaft sweat-box next door, previously a gay fuck-club called The Eagle Bar and actually part of Heaven itself, has played host to such seminal nights as Future, Troll and the Drum Club. Heaven can even be credited with creating its own form of music as it was here that Ian Levine, the club's founding DJ, built the sound of Boystown or HiNRG, a phoenix rising from disco's ashes.

Levine — who is most famous today as the brains behind post-Take That boy band, Bad Boys Inc — was responsible, more than anyone, for what Heaven became. A precocious Northern soul DJ from a well-off family, his

"In the beginning, God created Earth, and God said it was good. Then God created Man. And then Man created Heaven."

Stateside record-buying trips allowed him to explore the amazing underworld of New York's gay scene which was flourishing in the years following the Stonewall rebellion. Levine soaked up disco, produced records with legends like Tom Moulton, and visited clubs like 12 West, The Flamingo and Infinity, which he describes as "Like Heaven before Heaven existed."

"There was no sign just a black metal door, but inside it was like some sort of religious gathering, it was crammed to the rafters. and they were all blowing whistles and screaming I'd never seen this before." Within weeks, Levine had recreated this energy on the other side of the Atlantic, and Heaven was set for its place in history. After The Saint opened in New York in September 1980, a multi-million-dollar gay club based around a seventy-six foot aluminium dome, each city had a large and legal dancefloor on which their gay populations could enjoy unprecedented freedom. Levine flitting between the two, Heaven and The Saint evolved in parallel.

Levine left DJing when techno swept the gay scene. Laurence Malice, a promoter who had organised the dancers at Heaven, decided that it was time to launch something harder. Together with an unprecedented 24-hour license to allow dancing throughout the weekend (the not-yet-opened Ministry of Sound had received a similar license two weeks earlier), Trade, at Turnmills, gave many people their first taste of all-night off-the-planet abandon and forged the image of nineties gay clubbing — something which rapidly evolved into joyful and reckless pharmaceutical endurance.

"We were the first club in the country to popularise techno," Laurence remembers. "We played what we wanted and people had the choice to stay and enjoy themselves or go home. We educated gay people to a new sound. Mind you I can't fool myself, I think if we'd have played the usual Kylie soundtrack people would have still come just because of the novelty opening hours."

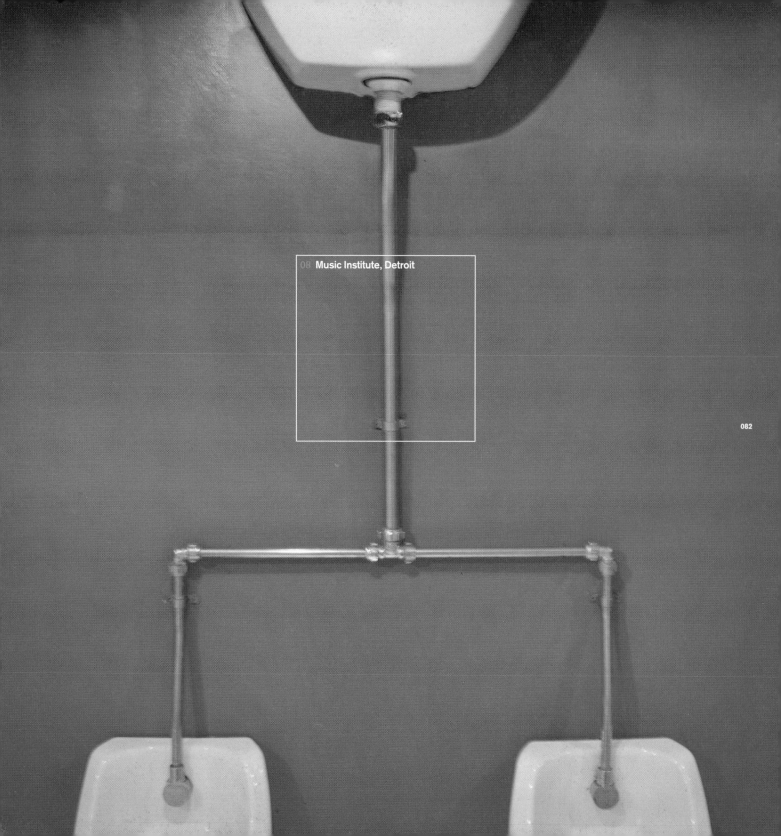

08 **Music Institute, Detroit**

"Today the car plants use robots and computers to make their cars, I'm more interested in Ford's robots than Gordy's music."
Juan Atkins

"The Techno Rebels will not vanish but will multiply in the years ahead," predicted Alvin Toffler in his 1980 book The Third Wave, imagining a class elevated from the masses by their mastery of high technology. This became a favourite text in the mythologies of the few who, between 1987 and 1991, made up the scene catalysed by Detroit's Music Institute. The Music Institute was Chez Damier's club, an all-night-and-most-of-tomorrow, no-alcohol bone-shaker sited in a retail building at 1315 Broadway, powered by Chez himself and by Detroit's techno triumvirate, Kevin Saunderson, Juan Atkins, and Derrick May. A medium-sized venue, holding about 400 people, the feelings it contained were very focused. "It was a spiritual place for music," remembers May. "We had a young, beautiful black crowd and I mean beautiful in the sense of spirit and soul. We had white kids coming, Spanish kids coming, gay kids coming, straight kids coming. Nobody was on drugs: kids smoked a little bit of weed, drank a little liquor, they came, had a ball, went home, made love and felt good feelings all week. I think there are only about four clubs in the world that can compare to its power and energy."

If Chicago in the eighties became a hotbed of musical creativity precisely because it combined musical tradition with comparative isolation, then it's no wonder that Detroit, an altogether more forgotten outpost, with a more recent musical past, produced techno. When Ford and General Motors brought the Motor City full employment, the soundtrack had been feelgood Motown; as continuing affluence brought black and white countercultures together, funk had fused with acid rock and given us Parliament-Funkadelic. Then, as the shrinking auto companies betrayed the population and made Detroit a post-industrial ghost-town, along came techno's moody cerebral futurism. "Today the automobile plants use robots and computers to make their cars. I'm more interested in Ford's robots than Gordy's music," said Juan Atkins, stressing how his city's desolate futuristic feel — and certainly not Detroit's Motown legacy — was techno's greatest inspiration.

Atkins, May and Saunderson, later to be known as the Belleville three after the high school they had all attended, were to become Detroit techno's most renowned originators. Atkins had been making Kraftwerk-inspired electro as Cybotron since the early-eighties. He introduced his friends to European electronic music and May and Saunderson reciprocated by taking him to Chicago's Music Box where DJ Ron Hardy was tearing down the walls with his explosive proto-house funk. The resulting collision of ideas produced electronic music of the most formalist austerity but still containing the emotional intensity of the most spiritual soul or gospel. Atkins became Model 500, Derrick May, as Rhythim Is Rhythim, released the seminal 'Nude Photo' and 'Strings Of Life', Kevin Saunderson released tracks as Reese and then formed Inner City and produced techno's vocal dance hits such as 'Big Fun' and 'Good Life'.

The city's economic desolation meant that the music was made largely for export. Despite techno having a great influence on the studios and dancefloors of Europe, the wider community of Detroit itself remained either ignorant or unsupportive of what was happening there musically. This isolation, however, made the tiny club scene even more special, and meant that the Music Institute played a huge role in directing the evolution techno would take. "The Music Institute is the key," recalls Carl Craig, remembering May DJing both there and on the radio. "He played the craziest edits of the wildest music. When Derrick DJed at the Institute you didn't know whether he was playing records or manipulating equipment. People would go crazy. Derrick would play 'Big Fun' three or four times and every time it blew my mind as well as everybody else's."

It's nine in the morning, sometime in 1991. Junior's been pumping the dancefloor since midnight and his famous siren has just marked a peak in the music. Dark bodies are dripping in the shadows; the people on the floor are moving with the steady power of a smooth machine. Everyone is loose with movement and focused on a single moment of existence; ready to continue this physical communion forever. Suddenly the half-light becomes darkness, the huge mirror ball is black, the Goddess of Light has plunged us into mystery. And the music stops. Dead.

In any other club, if the DJ tried anything like this, there would soon be a rustling of cigarette packets, a murmuring of voices, a stampede for the bar, but when Junior did it in the Sound Factory there was silence. Total respect. Awe. More than a thousand people stood bolt still in the dark, waiting for the thrill that they knew would follow. He would work the silence for several minutes, making bodies twitch with anticipation, teasing us with a growl or a squeak — a gentle touch to prepare you for an incredible sexual moment. He was letting everyone know that something amazing was about to happen. And then it did.

There was the time when the silence turned into saxophone thunder, to be broken by a Harley Davidson screaming across the dancefloor. Or the time they dropped dollar bills from the ceiling like snow, or the time that church organs fucked with our heads until we screamed for them to stop, or the time when Larry Levan had died and Junior made us all cry.

What made the Factory such an amazing place was the fact that it was big and it was pure. Until the tourists and the clueless started wandering in, around 1994, the people who went there formed a single-minded family. There was no alcohol, there were few girls, and there was no hint of the ugly outside world, just a huge simple room made small and intimate by the power of the music it contained.

Sound Factory was on 27th and Tenth, a dirty warehouse block patrolled by hookers and lowlife. You would file in around 4 or 5am, after a night's sleep, just as dawn was breaking; leaving the reality of New York's scuzzy concrete, to become enveloped in this bass cocoon. You were treated like an honoured guest: fruit, cookies, cold water and coffee were yours for free, there were hundreds of dollars worth of flowers gracing the entrance, and fresh decorations every week. At the exit there was always a huge bowl of condoms, and a pile of pencils and notepads to exchange phone numbers.

You would see incredible things there. Professional dancers would arrive from performing somewhere, and proceed to tear up a zone of the dancefloor. The voguing houses would be off in a corner, making catwalks along the side of the stage. Junior would grab a flashlight and pick out the more fabulous dancers, throwing down some bitch house track to exaggerate the competition.

In its heyday the faithful writhed and jumped till cramps and exhaustion set in. You were there for a seven or eight-hour workout, not a casual chat and a smoke along the sidelines. You only left the floor to visit the juice bar, the drinking fountain or the toilets. Nowhere in the Factory could you not hear the dancefloor.

Sound Factory opened on March 29th 1989 and finally closed its doors on January 12th 1995 after a hostile takeover of the building's lease (it reopened as Twilo several months later). Junior Vasquez is the DJ inextricably linked with the place, but Frankie Knuckles played there too, for a magical year from October 1990 to August 1991 and, amazingly, he happened to be there on the night it closed. "That was the last great room," he said. "There's not going to be anywhere like that again." Indeed, economic forces mean it is unlikely there will ever again be a truly underground club of such size and majesty. Those lucky enough to have been there were possibly the last to share the intimate communal experience of a single huge club built round a single DJ, open on a single night every week. Those days are gone. "It was the best club that I've ever been to," said Rocky of X-Press 2 when it closed, "The first time I went we were saying to each other, 'This is it, we've waited all our clubbing lives to be here tonight.'"

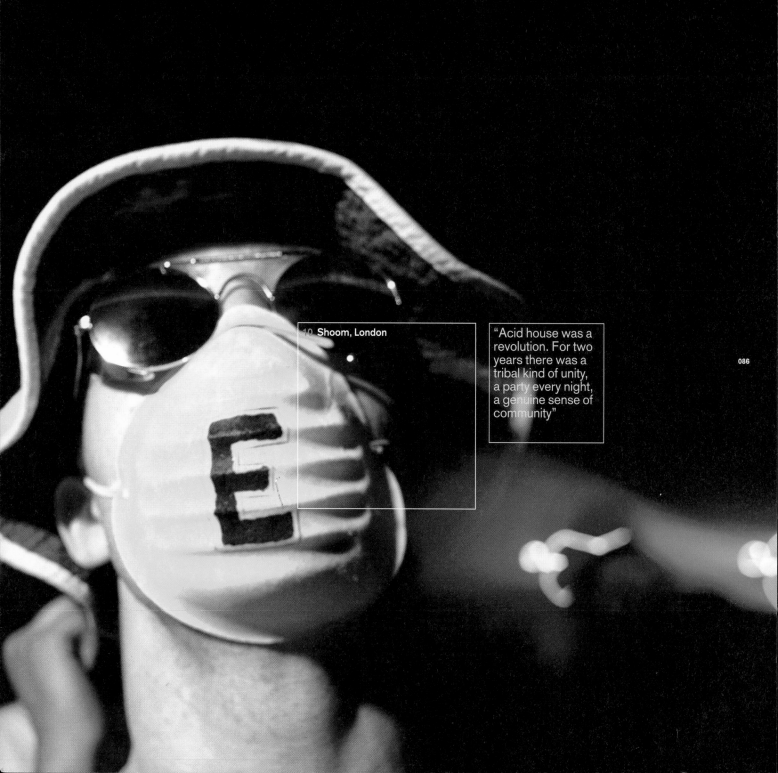

10 **Shoom, London**

"Acid house was a revolution. For two years there was a tribal kind of unity, a party every night, a genuine sense of community"

"Shoom, shoom, shoom. Are you feeling Shoomy?" laughed Trevor Fung, giggling at Danny Rampling on the dancefloor at Amnesia, Ibiza, shooming his way through a rushing peak in DJ Alfredo's gloriously wide-ranging music. The word stuck in Rampling's mind and when he and his future wife Jenni started a club to bring the island's sounds and spirit alive in London, this was the name they gave it. Started in mid-October 1987, Shoom was a turning point. It wasn't the first club where Ecstasy and acid house had come explosively together, but it was the first time they'd co-existed in a place that would get them noticed.

Oakenfold had Future and then Spectrum at Heaven, the first large-scale acid club, Nicky Holloway would take the music mainstream at the Trip at the Astoria, but Rampling's Shoom is the one on which it all hinged: the touchstone club where everything was in place. "It was innocence, a very happy and innocent time," he remembers. "We were trying to bring people together, that was our vibe."

Shoom started in The Fitness centre in Southwark Bridge Road SW1. Jon Marsh of The Beloved remembers hearing about, "this mad party going off in a gym". The friend who told him about it seemed scared by the intensity of the place. "He just didn't understand what was going on."

"It was a club where anything went," recalls Rampling. "Anybody that wanted to come along who had the right attitude was more than welcome. There was such a strong sense of freedom and no restrictions and that really appealed to a lot of people." Danny and Jenni set themselves the task of breaking what they saw as the cynicism of West End clubland. Testament to this is the broad mix of people who came to Shoom. In amongst the club kids and the suburban tearaways there were a sprinkling of 'faces', people like Martin Fry of ABC or Paul Rutherford of Frankie Goes To Hollywood. But in Shoom there was a sense of equality, and — for these clubland celebs — of anonymity. "It made for quite a unique feeling."

The club was so small that people would try to walk through the mirrors on the dancefloor's edge. Strobelights cut into strawberry-flavoured smoke onto the day-glo decorations and mad dancers in their baggy, utilitarian clothes — Converse trainers, dungarees or just jeans and a t-shirt — a look which was completely at odds with the style fascism that had long pervaded London. Later there would be bandannas and surfing shorts, smileys and fluorescent prints, an all-too-universal style which became disparagingly known as 'Acid Ted' by the original Shoomers ("Acieed", the war cry of the scene, was another later import from the more commercial clubs.) In their new state of non-alcoholic intoxication, the clubbers drank Lucozade and Perrier, which was initially given away free.

At a time when clubs were licensed only till two or three, Shoom stayed open until five or six in the morning. The music was Chicago house, especially the acid tracks which were rapidly multiplying. Rampling had a

show on Kiss FM (in those days a pirate station) and he recalls the tunes high on his post-Ibiza playlist: House Master Boyz' 'House Nation', Kenny 'Jammin' Jason's 'Can U Dance?', The Nightwriters' 'Let The Music Use You' and of course Phuture's 'Acid Trax'. There was some confusion at first because DJs like Carl Cox, who played the first night with Rampling, were still playing a lot of funk as well. "The first night was shaky but it was fun and the people enjoyed it," he remembers, "hence the enthusiasm to do it again a couple of weeks after." For the second Shoom, he booked Colin Faver, then London's most acid house intensive DJ. Faver went on to play more Shoom nights than anyone else, alongside Rampling himself, and others including Steve Proctor, Kid Batchelor, Mark Moore and Johnny Walker.

In keeping with Rampling's background, Shoom had a strong soul and garage undercurrent. In 1988, he begged Tony Humphries to come over to play. He also recalls a memorable PA with Robert Owens and Larry Heard. Oakenfold's Future was more eclectic, more truly Balearic thanks to Oakie's rock and hip hop credentials. Shoom also had more of a gay presence than Future.

For everyone who went there, including Danny himself, Shoom remains the source of some precious memories. "At the end of the night once I played 'Crusoe' by Art of Noise, an ambient track. We always used to bring the lights up bright and this guy just stepped out of the smoke and said, 'I've been on a spaceship'. People used to make us things, give us shirts they'd made, cards, tapes and records." He also recalls playing 'Give Peace A Chance' at the end of one night. "There's a photo of that with lots of people from clubland who are doing really good things now, just standing on the dancefloor with their hands held high together, joining hands."

Although it would have an incredible influence, the Shoom feeling was a fragile thing to protect. Many recall Jenni's ruthless door policy, seemingly at odds with the club's all-inclusive ethos, but simply an attempt to preserve the original atmosphere of the place. In the end Shoom moved to larger premises at the Tottenham Court Road YMCA and then to The Park in Kensington.

"Acid house was a revolution," believes Rampling. "For two years there was a tribal kind of unity, a party every night, a genuine sense of community. Even football violence almost disappeared. I think that really put the fear of God into the authorities, because a form of dance music succeeded where they'd failed so often. And Ecstasy did play a part. It changed a generation's outlook on things, and opened their minds. At least it did at first."

"I thought, this doesn't look too bad, I'll try one. Suddenly the whole place just sort of turned into this fabulous, sparkling colourful night"

Despite the rumours of a curse being placed on the island, Ibiza has long been known as a party destination. In the sixties many of Europe's jet-set, as well as disaffected hippies would congregate on the island, many choosing to stay thanks to its clement weather and laidback lifestyle.

In the early-eighties, a young London DJ, Trevor Fung, started visiting: "Around 1982 I went to work in Ibiza for a fellow called Felix who I used to work for in London. He used to own a club in Old Burlington Street called Fred & Ginger's and he also owned a club in Ibiza called Amnesia." Trevor had been going over there year after year, with a hardcore of British clubbers latching on to the special atmosphere engendered in clubs such as Pacha, Amnesia and Ku.

Meanwhile, a small clique of DJs had discovered a new style of music coming from Chicago and Detroit. One of them was Johnny Walker, then a resident at Frenchies in Camberley, one of the key clubs of the southern-eastern soul scene. "I started playing house at soul and jazz clubs to a horrific response. They just didn't understand it. I think I was playing things like Rhythim Is Rhythim's 'Nude Photo'." It was early days yet.

In the Summer of 1987, Walker, along with friends Paul Oakenfold (then mainly known as a hip hop man with a column in Blues & Soul), Danny Rampling and the organiser of Special Branch parties, Nicky Holloway, decided to go on a holiday to Ibiza. Principally out there for a break from London, they were stunned by what they found.

Walker remembers it well. "I think that Nightlife in San Antonio was the club where we were first offered an E. I was very hesitant at first, but having seen Paul and Danny and Nicky do one and then go skipping and hopping around the club holding hands going 'I love you', I thought well, this doesn't look too bad; I'll try one. And suddenly the whole night just sort of turned into this fabulous, sparkling colourful night. I just felt so wonderful." A forgivable naiveté overwhelmed them.

Before long they found themselves transported to Amnesia, where an Argentinian DJ by the name of Alfredo was resident. They walked into the open air club with its high white-walls, border of palm trees and a mirrored pyramid centre-stage. A wildly eclectic mix of people were in there dancing to a cacophonous mixture of records. "We were like, 'Wow! What the fuck is this?'," recalls Walker. "Alfredo was mixing up house records with indie guitar records, pop stuff like Madonna and George Michael, and then some of the things that are now balearic classics, that I suppose he was finding in Ibizan record shops."

It was a night that was to transform the contours of British clubbing forever. The equation of the right party, the right music and the right drug came together. And, although this formula had been made years before in a variety of places — Texas, New York and, of course, Ibiza — it was the will of this quartet to convert the world to their discovery that proved crucial.

The rest of the week was spent going to Amnesia to hear Alfredo. Paul Oakenfold obtained a tape of Alfredo's set and the four would sit by the pool during the day trying to work out exactly what the records were that he was playing: Woodentops' 'Why Why Why', 'Jesus On The Payroll' by Thrashing Doves, Carly Simon's 'Why', all mixed up with pop records and this new sound coming from Chicago and Detroit.

The effect on London was immediate. Nicky Holloway's Special Branch parties suddenly took on the veneer of the Balearics. Paul Oakenfold's Project Club in Streatham flew Alfredo over for after-hours parties, firstly with clubbers schooled in Ibiza's charms, but soon infecting a wider strata of clubgoers. Then came Shoom, the archetypal balearic/acid house jamboree. Johnny Walker remembers Rampling's first club well: "It was around November 1987 at the Fitness Centre in Southwark Street. It was, literally, a fitness centre downstairs with mirrored walls; it only held about 200. Everyone would turn up at midnight; get inside, lock the doors, and on with the smoke machines, strobes and the Balearic classics and the party would just go on until about six or seven in the morning."

In what seemed like weeks, Holloway had started a series of clubs at Astoria: Trip, Oranges Don't Dance, Made On Earth. Oakenfold had launched firstly Future, then Spectrum at Heaven (followed by Land of Oz). The Wag had Love; and there was Enter The Dragon in Kensington. The club explosion had started, swiftly followed by the first tabloid headlines about the 'Evil Acid Barons'.

Meanwhile, the Balearics continued to hold their special spell over people. Charlie Chester of Flying Records began to organise trips of clubbers over to the islands with British DJs — amongst them the original quartet — playing the circuit: Es Paradis, Pacha, Amnesia. A documentary on Ibiza appeared on Channel 4 entitled A Short Film About Chilling , it had Boy's Own, Happy Mondays et al soaking up the legendary sunsets.

While this was happening, a new club appeared on the club map. It's name was Space, originally a techno haunt, it gradually became more accessible, aided by its resident DJ Alex P, yet another British DJ entranced by the aura that surrounds the island. Perhaps more than any other club, Space provided the bridge between the Ibiza of legend and the Balearic island of today.

Gradually, the axis of night-time Ibiza began to rotate as more and more British holidaymakers visited the island and as British youth — the disenfranchised, the unemployed and the simply bored — came out to the island looking for fun in the sun, perhaps laced with a little work. UK promoters, sensing a golden opportunity, began to monopolise Ibiza's venues. The war of the superclubs that had been raging at home broke out 1,500 miles away: Ministry of Sound, Cream, Up Yer Ronson, Renaissance. In some ways it proved to be much more cut-throat even than in Britain, as evidenced by this quote from a UK promoter overheard

by a Muzik journalist: "Take those Miss Moneypennies posters down from there. We own that tree. That tree has been ours for the last three years." A small, largely unknown organisation known as Manumission (run by a pair of brothers, Andy and Mike), began to put on parties on the island that would increase the competition and provide them with unprecedented publicity. Using Ku (now known as Privilege) as their base, it was Manumission that created the current 'flyering' system, whereby each PR representing the club has their name on the flyers they hand out. Each flyer handed back at the door is worth £1 to the PR. This scheme, borne out of the poverty of its instigators, became the norm on Ibiza. Now, hundreds of people come over to San Antonio and Ibiza Town in the hope of finding one of these 'glamorous' jobs.

What brought Manumission its publicity, however, is nothing to do with flyers and everything to do with the weird menagerie of performers they brought to the island. The dwarves recruited from Paris, 'Alice' the transvestite (actually Big John, a systems engineer from Manchester), the people peeling potatoes and carrots in the middle of the dancefloor; or the man sat on a toilet in the club reading a paper, seemingly oblivious to his surrounds. Then, of course, there were the live sex shows performed by, amongst others, Mike Manumission and his partner Claire. At first this bacchanalian assault of the senses seemed a perfect cocktail of entertainment. By their own admission, they were not interested in DJs, or even the music. In fact, Manumission brought to mind Studio 54 in their abandonment of everything but their interest in the moment. Concept clubbing writ large.

As Manumission's increasingly tiresome antics continued to grab the headlines (by the end of the 1997 season, brothers Mike and Andy appeared to be diametrically opposed to each other), the other clubs got on with bringing nightlife-hungry clubbers sustenance based on music rather than live shagging. Ibiza 1997 was bigger than ever; the magic might have fundamentally altered, but it is still there for those sampling it for the first time.

Johnny Walker went out to Ibiza in 1997 for the first time in several years and noted a number of changes. "First of all, those beautiful open-air clubs, like Ku and Amnesia are covered now and that immediately changes the whole vibe and feeling you had then. The clubs now are mainly run by the British superclubs and they're full of British clubbers and nobody else. So, it's missing that colourful flamboyant excitement that the clubs had to offer. I even went to the clubs on non-British nights and, you know, where were the fan dancers at Pacha? Not there. Where were all the transvestites in Amnesia? Not there. It has undergone some changes and, for me, not for the better."

But what makes clubbing so special is its ability for renewal year after year. Sure, the original vibe has perhaps dissipated, but the same could be said for the UK's battle-weary clubs; and yet — like a snake shedding its skin — something new arrives each year to transform an otherwise moribund scene. Pacha, Space, Privilege and Amnesia still thrive. José Padilla, the ultimate chill-out DJ, still weaves his mesmerising spells at Café Del Mar. Are there better ways to spend an evening than watching the sun come down on another glorious Mediterranean day? Probably not.

13 Shelley's, Stoke-on-Trent

090

Amongst the many clubs swiftly elevated to the pantheon of 'classic' clubs, Shelley's Lazerdome is one that seems to have been overlooked. Perhaps the fact that it soared and crashed in a matter of months has something to do with it — it lasted a mere eighteen months in its entirety. Maybe its location, the deeply unfashionable suburb of Stoke-on-Trent known as Longton, accounts for part of this.

But it deserves to be remembered for a variety of reasons. Firstly, it helped create and establish Sasha's reputation. It also gave Dave Seaman, nowadays one of Kylie's producers, his first break in club DJing. In many ways, too, it was the prototype superclub (Renaissance's Geoff Oakes virtually lived there) though admittedly it didn't have much of the 'super' in physical evidence — the club itself was really nothing more than a chrome-plated 'Ritzy'-style venue. It could also justifiably claim to be the first northern handbag club. One thing is certain, however, for a few short months in 1990 and 1991, it was the place to party in the north-west.

Delight (as it was actually called) began in the late summer of 1990 when Mixmag photographer Gary McClarnan approached Sasha after Shaboo in Blackpool, where he had been playing, had closed down, and offered him a residency. The idea was for Sasha to do three Fridays and Dave Seaman the other, allowing Sasha to continue his commitments elsewhere. Seaman was at the opening night: "The first week was strange. There was a group of ravers all by the stage on the dancefloor and then by the bar were loads of Stoke City fans with scarves and shirts on, singing football songs. They were completely separate; there can't have been more than a couple of hundred in there."

At the time, the Haçienda was experiencing problems with Manchester's gangs (something which, predictably, would hasten the end of Shelley's too) and with Shaboo now closed, and limited choices elsewhere, it made perfect sense for ravers throughout the north-west to head for Longton on a Friday, something they did in increasingly large numbers. Within weeks the word had spread, and the football element had been squeezed out in favour of loved-up veterans of the rave scene.

Sasha's style of DJing was almost theatrical in its application. His love of the dramatic opening, the drawn-out intro, a cappellas carefully laid over minimal house tracks. Spatial sculptures of sound that drew the crowd in before hitting them with the renewed thud of bass. One of his mixes — Leftfield's 'Not Forgotten' underneath the a cappella of Whitney Houston's 'I Wanna Dance With Somebody' — became so well-known throughout the north-west, it was simply referred to as 'that Whitney mix'.

Dave Seaman, along with studio partner Steve Anderson, had already signed a deal with 4th & Broadway under the name Brothers In Rhythm. Their recording, 'Such A Good Feeling', went from Shelley's anthem to national charts. "'Peace And Harmony' was made for the Haçienda —

But it deserves to be remembered for a variety of reasons.

when I was going there every week — and 'Such A Good Feeling' was made for Shelley's. I would literally come back with all this 'artificial enthusiasm' and I'd be going 'we've got to do this and we've got to do that!'."

What made Shelley's special was the complete lack of planning. Making it up as you go along. It was what promoter, McClarnan believed it should be about. "Shelley's was called Lazerdome because it had this laser. It was notorious, mainly because the intense heat made it break down. It would be on for a while, it'd be quite fun, then it would stop working. We couldn't get it on for six months. Then the night it came on, when people saw it, they just went through the roof. And then it broke down again after a month!"

Such was the success of the club that after the 2am shutdown, everyone would head for Knutsford services on the M6. By the spring of 1991 the police — wise to what was going on — were blocking entry to it. Rave pranksters and local boys, Altern-8, helped put Shelley's on the map when they famously turned up on a truck outside the club in October 1991 whilst filming the video for 'Activ-8'. Intending to do two tracks, the crowd demanded more and it was only when police offered to relieve them of their lorry that the impromptu gig came to an end. (McClarnan reckons they only did it because they couldn't get a gig at the club.)

Not long after, famed Friday night, Delight came to a sticky end too. Those involved put it down to a mixture of gangs gradually muscling in, naiveté on their part and horrendous drug-consumption. Promoter McLarnan did not step in another club for two years after Shelley's ended and has not taken drugs since. In youth magazine, Young People Now, he admitted, "I was taking five times as much as everyone else. Because everyone used to takes Es as tablets, we'd do something else and snort it. I was an addict definitely." Thankfully, McClarnan, though shaken, is as articulate and sanguine now as he had been originally. "I do feel that if Shelley's hadn't happened, you wouldn't have got people travelling to clubs and places like Cream and Renaissance wouldn't have happened. We spent a lot of time with Geoff [Oakes, of Renaissance], and I think Shelley's was influential in him starting a club night."

A 117-mile ribbon of tarmac snaking through the countryside of the home counties, Berks and Bucks, Herts and Hants, passing endless fields, cowsheds, aircraft hangars, places where the spirit of dance brought thousands together in pagan communion. Sunrise, Biology, Back To The Future, Energy, Raindance: names that conjure tribal rituals in faraway places, hinting at secret musical shamanism. The M25 was completed in 1988, countless hundreds of acres of four lane blacktop. If you're nostalgic for a car-jam there exists a 103-minute video of a complete circuit. As the eighties turned nineties however, the M25 became more than just a big ugly road, it was a means to a party explosion, the highway to heaven.

The London orbital motorway was one of the factors which made raves possible, mobile phones were another, as was British Telecom's multi-line Voicebank messaging service. However, more important than all of these was the spirit of the time — the feeling which countless burnt-out ravers will evoke with misty-eyed nostalgia — the spirit of togetherness. A rave was an idealised version of clubbing. It wasn't about visiting some purpose-built place, it was about creating somewhere new; it was about building a city for a night — a dream city of friendly strangers. A club had a venue, a place in space and time, but a rave was all about possibilities. A rave existed in the minds of the people who danced together. Without them it was nowhere, just a field off a motorway exit. Raves emphasised the Ecstatic acid house ideal: it was people that counted above everything. A rave was always about community, joining you to the four or five friends who made up your carload, to the ten or twenty cars that realised they were all heading the same way, to the hundreds and thousands of people who shared a dancebeat, and, if the drugs were right and the gods were happy, shared an experience of communion like none had ever felt before. It was a reward for the hard work of gaining entrance: beating police roadblocks, lurking in service stations, calling with a cellphone (or a coinbox if you weren't so flash) for the ground zero, tracking the bassline until you found the site.

Memories are sharp from this time. People recall the shock of seeing so many people 'losing it' together, they remember feeling that they'd discovered a new way for people to behave towards each other. No-one knew if the police would arrive, no-one knew who was DJing and no-one cared, no-one knew if the next track would be a teeth-grinding acid monster or a swooping dream of euphoric vocals. In the true spirit of music and dance they were truly in the moment.

All this is to ignore the fact that large fortunes were made from the rave explosion, and that much of the motivation for their creation was undoubtedly financial. Certainly, after the initial parties, a cynical opportunism was quickly to the fore. But even sharp operators like Tony

The M25 became more than just a big ugly road: it was the means to a party explosion

Colston-Hayter, the man behind the earliest events including Sunrise and Back To The Future, possessed at least a degree of sympathy for the ideals which raves came to represent.

After clubbing at Shoom and Spectrum, in the summer of 1988 Colston-Hayter began organising warehouse parties, including several in Wembley Studios which he called Apocalypse Now. The Shoomers experimented with outdoor parties, taking clubbers on buses out to a farm and filling a barn with fire-engine foam. With the success of big clubs like Spectrum and then Trip, the possibilities of ever larger venues looked exciting. But when the tabloids ran a story about 'acid' dealers in Spectrum, roping Richard Branson, one of the owners of Heaven, into the scandal, it was obvious there would be a lot of unwelcome interest. Colston-Hayter saw the need for some dramatic changes: "I thought, I want to get out of London altogether so it doesn't disturb people and there isn't a huge police presence."

After his Wembley parties, Colston-Hayter put together Sunrise, The Mystery Trip. On 22nd October 1988 ten coaches ferried clubbers from the BBC studios in west London to an equestrian centre in Buckinghamshire. Passengers included most of the acid scene's club promoters as well as stars including Martin Fry, Andrew Ridgely and Boy George. They arrived to see strobe lights and flaming torches lighting up the sky and then, plunged into darkness except for a single laser, heard Steve Proctor play a set which started with the apocalyptic theme from 2001. "It was the beginning of the orbital parties," recalls Colston-Hayter. "In the morning everyone was outside dancing. All the Shoom kids were getting flowers and putting them in their hair and talking to all the horses, like they'd never seen a horse before. Some kids started walking home, they thought they'd get home eventually."

Later parties expanded the possibilities, and as well as ever more grandiose productions — huge sound systems, amazing lasers and lightshows, even funfair rides — the promoters learnt quickly the value of mailing lists, mobile phones, reprogrammable telephone message lines (to keep the address secret until the last minute), and the importance of having several possible venues and speedy construction. Incredible scams were pulled off to secure sites and to deflect police interest. And in the early days, the police weren't always the killjoy ogres of legend. Colston-Hayter recalls cops at Sunrise 4000 ferrying ravers from the car-park field to the event in their van, one of them even wearing a smiley on his helmet. Also contrary to the established folklore, raves weren't isolated to the home counties. Some spectacular events were brought off around Manchester, especially those around Blackburn which launched the career of Alexander Coe, aka Sasha.

Things got bigger 4,000, 5,000, 10,000 people would gather as the promoters perfected their methods and the word spread. In summer 1989 the movement peaked. At a Biology event in 1989, Johnny Walker recalls playing for 12,000 ravers, "It was breathtaking, to be on stage and look out and see that many people dancing to what you're playing, it was just incredible." Eventually, however, the momentum died. It was killed, not only by police over-reaction to the lurid tabloid tales of drug dealing at raves, but also because there were a few too many disappointments. Unscrupulous promoters tried to become overnight millionaires by selling tickets to imaginary events, and ravers were soon used to events that delivered a tenth of what they promised. Also, by this time the club scene had expanded to accommodate the huge numbers of clubbers who had been turned on by the acid house explosion. There was little reason to spend the night driving round unlit highways in search of a party that probably didn't even exist. By the time the government moved against raves, in the form of the 1990 Entertainments (Increased Penalties) Act, much of the excitement had already gone.

It took a long time before the idea of legal raves took hold, although as the focus for the hardcore and breakbeat movement, the scene gathered steam after about 1992 and was once more host to some spectacular events: Fantazia, Vision, Obsession, Raindance, Roast, Dreamscape, Helter Skelter, Jungle Fever, Ravelation, Telepathy, World Dance, and latterly Hardcore Heaven Tazmania and United Dance. Rave peaked commercially in 1993 with crowds of up to 25,000 at Fantazia and Vision events. But 1997 found the movement on its knees. Wax magazine bemoaned the death of the scene lost, it argued, to violent security, disorganised production, the reluctance of the authorities to grant licenses and most of all to competition from clubs and the falling age of the ravers themselves with the consequent lessening of their spending power. Raving was always about being a participant and about enduring hardship in order to find fun. It's easy to argue that once raves were legalised and mass-marketed, the amount of input from the punter was too small and they were little more than enormous club nights. Some of the first rave generation find solace in the big annual music festivals, but most are content to muse wistfully about the days when a traffic jam could start you rushing.

THE ANNUAL I
Mixed by Pete Tong & Boy George

14 Ministry of Sound, London

Maybe it's because the UK is a small place. Maybe it's because there weren't that many precedents. Or maybe it's because we don't have the vision, or the money, or the guts. Whatever it is, purpose-built large pleasure palaces like the Haçienda, Heaven or the one in question here, the Ministry of Sound, do not get built every day.

Predictably — like Haçienda and Heaven before it — the Ministry was inspired by New York clubs. In particular, the Paradise Garage for its sound system and atmosphere, and Area for its monthly changing themes. There were three people essential in setting the whole thing up: Justin Berkman (for the concept), James Palumbo (for the dough) and Humphrey Waterhouse (for making things happen). Berkman, then a largely unknown mouthy young DJ recently returned from a life-changing spell in New York, had been to the Paradise Garage and knew that this was what London needed. Dave Piccioni, an English DJ who had made it big in New York, remembers Berkman approaching him after the pair had returned home to the UK. "He said that he was going to build a club like the Garage. People were always saying this, so I was just like, 'Yeah, okay, Justin'."

But Berkman was a man on a mission and, after a few false starts (including putting a bid in for the basement of TGI Fridays in Covent Garden), the Gaunt Street site was found. "We'd nearly given up," says Berkman. "I remember I was driving home at night and I saw the front and thought 'that looks wicked; that's the place'. The whole point of the club was that it had to be interesting; had to have flavour; had to be really cool. So we got in to look around and saw it was just being used to park six cars and a dozen pigeons."

The building work for the Ministry was completed in twelve frantic weeks, including a specially built roof to contain the sound system which had 140 dB(A) capability — roughly equivalent to Concorde taking off ten feet away. The system itself was provided by associates of Richard Long the man that made the sound system for the Paradise Garage (Long himself died in the mid-eighties). Berkman was adamant about the priorities: "My concept for the Ministry was purely this:100% sound system first, lights second, design third — in that order — the reverse of everyone else's idea." A 24 hour dance license was secured at the eleventh hour and MoS was in business.

095

"My concept for the Ministry was purely this:100% sound system first, lights second, design third - in that order - the reverse of everyone else's idea."

Justin Berkman

Dave Piccioni was invited to the opening of the club: "I can remember walking into the entrance of the club and thinking, 'this looks just like the Garage'. Then I walked into the bar and the dance area. I thought, 'Fuck me, he did it.'"

The Ministry built its early reputation on two things: a magnificent sound system and top American DJs. Up until then, the Americans had been coming over, but only on an ad hoc basis (Levan and Kevorkian at Moist; Humphries at Shoom; a few early tours). MoS brought them all over: Carpenter, Clivilles and Cole, Levan, Knuckles, Morales, Kevorkian and Tenaglia. An almost endless list, in fact.

By his own admission, Berkman's arrogance alienated people, but as dance music was rapidly growing in the UK, he thought that what was needed was some instruction from America. "I felt that there were a lot of DJs playing the game without the rulebook. If I could get these guys over they could educate the DJs, the crowd, the works. They created the sound and they could teach us. I got Levan over and he taught me so much. What he taught me was sound. I was playing some bollocks before Levan came on and I really didn't know what I was doing. The first track was 'Should Have Been You' by Gwen Guthrie and the sound system sounded like it had previously been switched off and he switched it on. It was that clear; that much of a difference. The sun came out."

The continuing success of the Ministry has been its ability to adapt and change to the mood of clubland at any given time. Its highly successful Friday night, Open, has given, under the aegis of Jim Masters, to one of the finest UK dance labels. Its Saturday nights have continued to evolve without forsaking its black American roots with DJs such as Tony Humphries, CJ Mackintosh, Jazzy M, Jon Marsh enjoying extended residencies alongside the cream of US and European garage music jocks. Whatever else the Ministry organisation concerns itself with these days, its club will always be the pivot around which all else revolves.

The DJs

097

01. Larry Levan

There are no DJs, living or otherwise, who have had such potent mythology constructed around them as Larry Levan. His tragically premature death in 1992 signalled the end of a remarkable career that still casts a shadow over the dance community. Talk to any New York DJ of a certain age about music and it's likely that Levan's name will be mentioned in the first ten minutes. He is widely quoted as being the greatest modern DJ, whilst the club that he presided over for ten years — the Paradise Garage — is held in equally high regard.

Born in Brooklyn in 1954, Levan got his break in 1972 when the DJ at the club where he worked, the Continental Baths, was sacked. The owner told him to go to home and get some records, "It was Memorial Day weekend," Levan recalled. "I went back to Brooklyn and borrowed records from my friend Ronnie Roberts, who had everything. I went back and worked three straight days." After spending over a year at the Baths, a friend, Richard Long (who would later construct the mighty Garage sound system, as well as Frankfurt's techno club, Dorian Gray), invited him to start a night together, the Soho Club on Broadway. After losing that space, they moved to 143 Reade Street where his reputation was swelling. "I started working there and it got so crowded I just used to open the window and let the sound go out on the street. When the club had to close because of overcrowding, they asked me not to play anywhere else until the new club opened".

That new club was the Paradise Garage. A huge warehouse-like space that had been converted from a garage into a members-only club. It partially opened in 1977 with only the smaller room open (they didn't have sufficient funds to finish it) and a sound system that had been specifically designed by Levan and collaborator Long. What made Levan so special was his understanding of drama and how to create it, with pauses between discs, sound effects or later, with his collaborator on Peech Boys project, Michael DeBenedictus, on live keyboards. He understood space as much as music — he was a great fan of dub reggae, and often played productions by Jamaican rhythmatists, Sly & Robbie. His genius was a great ear for music, often displaying bewilderingly eclectic tastes; telling stories through his sets. As DJ Benji Candelario remembers: "The thing about Larry was he played like he was in your living room. He played all types of music, whether it was 98 bpm or 130 bpm; he didn't care so long as he captured that vibe. Technically, he wasn't a good DJ, but he was a great programmer."

From disco classics like MFSB's 'Love Is The Message' to unreserved rock freakouts like Steve Miller Band's 'Macho City', Levan threw the lot into the Garage melting pot creating a stirring brew of rhythmic intensity. Levan was the original balearic DJ before most people even knew where the Balearics were.

Levan not only made his mark as a DJ, his studio stints amply demonstrated a progressive mind at work, too. From his earliest remixes ('Got My Mind Made Up' by Instant Funk, Dee Dee Bridgewater's 'Bad For Me') through to his work with Bernard Fowler and DeBenedictus as New York Citi Peech Boys, Levan showed the same stripped-down dubwise mentality that producers such as François Kevorkian and Arthur Russell had shown with their work. The Peech Boys' 'Don't Make Me Wait' and 'Something Special' were both Garage favourites as well as becoming great records in their own right elsewhere ('Don't Make Me Wait' was a minor pop hit in the UK), whilst mixes such as Taana Gardner's 'Heartbeat', with its stripped-to-the-rhythm approach, pre-empted (and prompted) the house sound.

Levan's physical decline began well before the Garage closed in 1987 and continued as he guested at clubs around both the city and, by that stage, the world. "We brought him over for three days," recalls Ministry of Sound co-founder, Justin Berkman. "He stayed for three months. He arrived eight days late with no records. I was like, 'Larry, where are your records?' He said, 'I haven't got any.' 'No records?' 'I've sold them all'. He had a massive heroin problem at that stage and he'd regularly do his wages in gear before he finished playing. And he'd sell his record collection on a regular basis. His friends would go to the market and see it for sale: buy it back and he'd re-sell it. In the end they gave up."

Shortly before his death, he went on a tour of Japan with François Kevorkian, who remembered it thus: "Larry went into a set of Philadelphia classics which was just so poignant, so emotional because the message of all the songs said he was really hurting. We all felt it at the time, but I think he pretty much knew he was dying and all the songs he played were so deeply related to how fast life goes. He played Jean Carne's 'Time Waits For No-one' and The Trammps' 'Where Do We Go From Here', and I realised that this was one of the best moments of greatness that I had ever witnessed in my life. It was so obvious, so grand, such a drama to it, that you just knew."

Levan died two months later in November 1992. Each July on his birthday, a remembrance party is held in New York for him with old Garage DJs like David Depino holding court, a testament to the influence he has exerted over dance music in general and New York in particular.

099

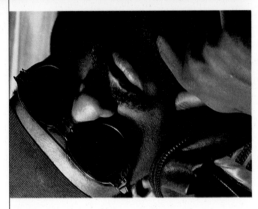

04. Afrika Bambaataa

"I'm trying to bring the world's music under one roof," says Bam. "One nation under a groove." As the founder, in 1974, of The Universal Zulu Nation, Afrika Bambaataa ('affectionate chief') is the revered old king of hip hop culture, giving continuity to its many splintered facets. A former gang leader from the Bronx, he began his DJing career following closely behind hip hop pioneer Kool Herc, and shot to fame in 1982 with a record named after his real home 'Planet Rock', easily one of the most influential records ever. This spliced the essence of Kraftwerk together with the cut-up scratch DJing which he had helped evolve, and formed the funky foundation of electro… and then house… and hip hop… As a DJ, Bambaataa's sets are unique in their diversity. Techno and drum and bass next to Italian house and an old Public Enemy classic is quite normal. But don't ask him about the aliens.

03. Boy George

He's seen it all has George. Having risen from humble origins in south-east London, he became one of the dandy stalwarts of the late seventies/early eighties Blitz scene — later to develop into the fashion disaster known as new romanticism. By 1982, as singer with Culture Club, he had scored his first UK no. 1 with 'Do You Really Wanna Hurt Me?'. Less then six months later he duplicated its success in the US. Hit single after hit single followed. So did drug addiction.

By the mid-eighties, George was better known by his regular appearances in the gutter press for various drug-related misdemeanours than for his music. Normally, right about now, the woeful tale of a life tragically cut short would unfold. But not with Boy George.

Pulling back from the brink, he reinvented himself firstly as the pop-mystic Jesus Loves You, creating Balearic classic (and pop smash) 'Generations of Love'; then as party DJ extraordinaire, unafraid of throwing any old disco tune as long as it brought a smile to his face and a whoop from the crowd. Between all of this, he also wrote one of the funniest, saddest and most revealing autobiographies ever written by a pop star.

Jesus Loves You, George, and so do we.

04. Derrick Carter

A DJ since the age of nine, happy pup Derrick Carter rose to fame as the ambassador of the city's mid-nineties renaissance. When house hit, he was a suburban youngster captivated by the legendary Hot Mix 5 radio shows. "Us Chicago kids thought we were listening to a different music from anyone else on the planet." His teenage job as a buyer in the Imports Etc record store let him get the hottest tracks from Europe before anyone else and gave him a link to the underground Black gay scene of Frankie Knuckles and Ron Hardy. He honed his phenomenal technical talent throwing huge spontaneous loft parties. Derrick has close connections to London and Detroit, but his music, which combines the city's hard beat tracks with a love for the classics of house and disco to make a progressive crystalline mix of techno and garage, is unmistakably a product of the Windy City.

Go on Pete, laaarge it! Who's got the power? Pete Tong's got the power! It's fair to say that Pete Tong is not the best DJ in the world. He has never wandered off into production like many of his peers. His DJ sets do not have journalists and fellow rocks salivating with anticipation. And yet, thanks to his Radio One show and position as head of A&R at London Records, he is the most famous product of the UK's explosion of DJs. If the readers of the quality press could name one DJ, it would probably be Pete Tong. If the glossy magazines want a quote on a dance issue of the day, it usually comes from the erudite chops of Tong, too. His name has even entered into the rich pantheon of Cockney rhyming slang (as in: it's all gone a bit Pete Tong). So in the words of his show: who's got the power?

Pete Tong was born in Dartford in 1960. He attended public school where he became first a drummer then — after he saw that DJing seemed more fun and was much less hard work — a DJ. He first began to make his mark as one of the young guns of the Soul Mafia, a loose collective of south-east based DJs that included the likes of soul veteran Robbie Vincent (along with several others who have since progressed into A&R departments at leading majors).

Having run a mobile disco in his home county of Kent for a while after he left school, he joined Blues & Soul magazine as an advertising rep in 1979. By the time he left in 1983, he was features editor. His departure was brought about by a job offer from London Records. At the time it was a well-established part of Dutch multinational Polygram, with hundreds of hits under its belt, from the pop frippery of Bananarama to the first ever house compilations, 'House Sound Of Chicago'. Fifteen years on, Tong is still there.

Although Tong's career has followed a smoothly skywards trajectory, it was his discovery of house music and his subsequent championing of the new sound that established him as a major force. "I got into house in 1986, when I was in New York," he remembers. "Some friends of mine tipped me off on a record by Sleazy D and one by JM Silk. I shot up to Chicago and met Rocky Jones from DJ International and Larry Sherman from Trax." Along with the compilations, he licensed key records from the burgeoning scene in Chicago (the first crossover record, 'Love Can't Turn Around' and the first number one, 'Jack Your Body', both came out on London. Orbital was also an early signing). His position of preeminence was confirmed when he took over from long-standing mentor Jeff Young as the presenter of Radio One's specialist dance show in 1991 (he had already replaced Young at his two previous stations: Radio London and Capital). For spoiled inhabitants of the big cities (especially London with its myriad pirates), the show may not seem a big deal. For those less fortunate, it has been a lifesaver, a link to the outside world and a chance to hear tunes months before anyone else will have them. Pete Tong's Essential New Tune can make or break a record, and it has made plenty.

On the surface, Pete Tong is the archetypal ordinary bloke, in no small part the key to his success. Yet there is nothing ordinary about him. Beneath the studied smile, lies the iron resolve of the successful A&R man. As a DJ — both on radio and in clubs — Tong is not a chancer; he rarely goes out on a limb to break records. And yet he always seems to perfectly judge the right moment to introduce a new record, or a new style of music (it's no coincidence that drum and bass's breakthrough artist, Goldie, is ensconced on London). "When jazz funk was in, I was playing jazz funk. When hip hop was breaking, I was playing hip hop. That's what I try and reflect in the radio show: whatever's happening. If suddenly a new form of music comes in tomorrow, I'm not gonna make it 100% of my show; I'll filter it in."

Few people get close to him and, despite the reams written about Tong, still very little is known about who he really is. But one thing's for certain: he has got the power.

06. Gilles Peterson

One of the apprentices of the UK's jazz-dance movement of the mid-eighties (the main men were Baz Fe Jazz and maverick Paul Murphy), Gilles Peterson has survived several fads and movements, ending in triumph when the act he had nurtured, Roni Size & Reprazent, scooped the Mercury New music award in 1997 with their groundbreaking mélange of drum and bass fused with modern soul. It was a victory against all odds both for A&R man Peterson and for Roni Size himself, one which vindicated his stubborn approach to the music he believes in.

A soul boy from an early age, his stints on pirate station Radio Invicta gave him a voice on the claustrophobic London club scene. Gigs at Nicky Holloway's Special Branch parties followed. In the late eighties he helped set up the Acid Jazz label, putting out records by acts on the then burgeoning scene (which had become known by the same name as his label). His Sunday afternoon sessions — Talkin' Loud Saying Something — down at Camden's seedy rock joint, Dingwalls, cemented his reputation as one of the south-east's most eclectic jocks, with early hip hop and house tracks nestling neatly between the Latin-jazz lite of Flora Purim. "As a DJ it was the best club I've ever done," he reflected later, "because I felt it was a club that was open to everyone. It didn't have the West End's restrictions and door policies. The music was incredibly mixed."

In 1989, he was approached by Polygram about the possibility of setting up a jazz-oriented stable. Talkin' Loud, the label, was born. In truth Talkin' Loud struggled badly for the first few years after the early departure of the man who had brought Peterson to Polygram. Realistically, the acts he had brought to the label had a limited constituency aside from the goatee-strokers and jazz snobs of the suffocatingly trendy London scene. However, in 1991 he hit a run of form when three acts had chart hits within a two month span (the Young

Disciples' 'Apprently Nothin'', Omar's 'There's Nothing Like This' and 'Always There' by Brit-funk veterans Incognito). Despite this, the accusations of clique-ishness were rife. Two things were to alter his approach to both A&R and DJing. The first was a record produced by Masters At Work called 'The Nervous Track' by Nuyorican Soul on NY indie label, Nervous. Although nominally a house record, it dispensed with a four/four kick in favour of a jazzily syncopated breakbeat. It sounded like James Blood Ulmer's harmolodics thrown in the tumble dryer with Marshall Jefferson. Peterson (by now on Kiss FM) wore the grooves down on his treasured copy and asked Masters At Work if they

would be interested in making an album based around the Nuyorican concept. They signed to Talkin' Loud, and released an acclaimed LP in 1997.

The second was his discovery of the emerging drum and bass scene and in particular a club called 'Speed' where LTJ Bukem was resident. "That club really turned my life around. I really felt like I'd found my roots again and escaped the bubble I was in. " As a result, both Roni Size and the up and coming 4 Hero were signed to the label. His latest club, the Monday night jamboree that is That's How It Is re-affirms his commitment to his anything-goes policy.

Todd, they say, is God. And as God, he is, of course, omnipotent and omnipresent — way more fun than just playing records. He has a reputation for ego and he likes to leave people thinking that he might be a bit of a gangster, but as the man who commands the highest price-tag for a session behind the decks, as someone who can make a party rock with no records except his own, as the pioneer producer credited with making house hard — adding some armed-and-dangerous Brooklyn bounce to the sounds coming out of Chicago, Todd Terry is entitled to his little spells of arrogance.

If you ask what motivates him, he'll say something like 'Battling people'. He'll tell you, like a bragging homeboy, "I got to beat everybody. It's me against every DJ and producer that's in house."

Raised in Brooklyn, in the crumbling seaside neighbourhood of Coney Island, Todd started by DJing hip hop, working with acts like The Jungle Brothers, back in the days when 'hip-house' was the future. When he started making records, using the name Masters At Work (used more famously by his friends Louie Vega and Kenny Gonzalez), his productions stressed the Latin sound of freestyle, but then, as the music of Chicago began to filter across the world, he took that early house sound and added a New York edge, throwing in complex rhythms with a Latino influence and ending up with his trademark hard, percussive funkiness. "That Chicago sound. I took it to the next level. It was a whole different thing," he says. "I tried to put a hard flavour to everything, tried to give some type of drive. You'd listen to it and say "Only Todd would do that, that's Todd's drum pattern, that's his sound, the dark wild type sound.'"

Songs like Royal House's 'Can You Party', and Todd Terry Project's 'Weekend', and 'Bango', among the first house records to break over here, were what brought him UK

been consolidated with a steady stream of underground tracks, high-profile remixes, and the occasional monster dance hit. Most producers remember being inspired by great records. Todd insists he makes music because he hears too many awful ones. "My thing is don't waste vinyl," he says. "I try to make every record a classic." Surprisingly, despite being key to house music history, he will often declare that hip hop is still where his heart lies. And sitting in a studio, his backward cap topping off his dark moon(?) face, he reminds you of

nothing more than a big bad B-boy. He's cocky, self-assured, ready to do battle, and he doesn't really care what other people think. He makes money, he makes great records while he's at it, and like a tough, swaggering homeboy, he dreams big dreams about huge success and living large. Producers making bad records? "I'm gonna take them out." The music business? "Too much bullshit." And Todd Terry's idea of success? "If I make the money I wanna make, I'm just gonna hang out and laugh at people

08. Sven Väth

Trancemeister Sven Väth (say "Fayt") was such a notorious bon viveur that at his 1995 velocity his friends jokingly gave him only ten years to live. Frankfurter Sven had been known to drink fifty-eight beers in a single DJing set, however, his sets of mesmerizing Wagnerian techno can last up to thirty hours. Such epic marathons, captured on vinyl on the crucial 'Accident In Paradise' LP, helped define European trance and earned him a following of fanatic baldies, some of whom even sport tattoos of his name. Recently he has slowed down, both in music and in lifestyle. He declared trance was now boring, parted company with his labels Harthouse and Eye-Q and saw his club, The Omen in Frankfurt, close. He spun there for nine years as well as enjoying a parallel residency at The Orbit in Leeds. With more spare time, Sven will continue such nutty behaviour as dancing naked around a candlelit room while supposedly being interviewed or dressing up as a raven for the Love Parade, Berlin's 24-hour open-air techno festival.

09. Andy Weatherall

Been there, seen that, got the badge. Andy Weatherall, former captain of the Good Ship Balearic, has been places most of us only dream about, yet still maintains the spikey punk outlook of his youth. As a member of the Boy's Own collective, he co-produced their anarchic club and footie 'zine, Boys Own, before winding up as a DJ at the legendary Shoom. Production work also took off after he transformed Primal Scream's 'I'm Losing More Than I'll Ever Have' into one of the signature records of the blissed-out beginning of the decade — the Peter Fonda-sampling 'Loaded'.

He followed this by starting a band, Bocca Juniors, who produced a pair of now sought-after tunes, 'Raise' and 'Substance', and started DJing sets that became harder and more confrontational as the decade progressed and cynicism set-in. Perhaps something to do with his punk roots. In the midst of this, he set up a club (Sabresonic) which delivered some seriously stonking music, and another band (Sabres of Paradise) which delivered some seriously skanking music, with their tune 'The Theme' making it on to TV accompanying a Bacardi ad.

Predictably, just when it looks like Weatherall's heading for a bigger stage, he junks the programme. In 1996, he began a new label, Emissions Audio Output, and a new act, Two Lone Swordsman, dedicated to trawling deeper sounds.

10. Josh Wink

"I never take drugs, so I guess even without any help my mind has always been left of the norm," laughs Philadelphia's groove-trance gentleman Josh Wink, one of the most level-headed people in dance who nevertheless produces some of the weirdest, tripped-out music available. Dreadlocked Joshua Winkelman learned his craft as a wedding DJ but by 1988 was a chiselled cycle courier by day and promoter of Philly's first rave-style warehouse parties by night. He found fame via enthusiastic globetrotting DJing and by making a chart-busting series of seriously mind-altering trance singles, in particular, 'Higher States Of Consciousness'. 'Don't Laugh' was the tune that led the way — nine minutes of (his own) acid-processed maniacal laughter. 'I'm Ready' then took snare rolls to new lengths and set DJs worldwide the impossible task of finding a record to follow it. He is one of the few DJs that dance-ignorant America has heard of and if you were putting money on someone to drag the US scene out from the underground depths, Josh Wink would be your best bet.

The Big Guy. Dance music's Mr Nice. Ol' Three-Decks Cox. Easy-going. Top bloke. These are all epithets that have been applied to Carl Cox, the UK's most popular DJ. All of them fit, of course, but Carl Cox is much more than just a good guy. He's the guy who was there at the start, playing clubs like Shoom and the Project, appearing on Top of the Pops with his crossover tune 'I Want You Forever', released on Perfecto in 1991. He was hardcore's Mr Big for a while but, resenting the tag, swiftly re-invented himself as a techno DJ (breakbeat man, DJ Seduction once said when he met him, "I can't believe you've left us and that you're playing all this intelligent bollocks now").

That's the thing about Cox. Just when you think you've got him pegged, he confounds your expectations. Take his Kiss FM show. Now largely known as a techno jock, Cox spent the first hour of his show playing a brew of rare grooves, classic disco and house foundations. As he saw it: "People need to be educated about how dance music got like it is today. I wanted to show people there was life before house and techno."

A suburbanite, Cox first played with a mobile disco in the early eighties (his first regular gig was at Sutton United FC's social club), before breaking on to the guest DJ circuit in Brighton and London. Cox played at the first two Shooms, then was summarily dismissed — something which, from subsequent interviews, obviously still rankles. No matter. It wasn't long before he had established himself as one of the country's premier rave DJs, with his reputation as a dexterous deckmeister second to none. "In those days he could mix a record in four seconds flat," recalls a fellow DJ. "He seemed to mix it up more than anyone else would." At his peak, he

was playing to thousands of punters every week at huge outdoor raves like Sunrise. The inevitable record deal followed, swiftly followed by disillusionment. The aforementioned chart hit brought pressures on Cox which pulled him further and further away from his roots in the clubs. He was dropped.

In 1993 he took another major leap into the unknown when he forsook the clubs and the music he was playing for a back-to-basics approach. The name Carl Cox began to appear on flyers, prefaced by 'house set'. He took a big cut in wages, as well as vilification on the scene he had helped build. It paid off. This phase reached its apotheosis with 'The End Of

The Cliché', an LP on his own Ultimatum label. While not universally loved by critics, Cox sees it as a personal statement as much as anything else: "It was just how I felt at the time. It was made at an emotional period for me."

Not content to rest on his laurels, he has set up a weekly club night in London, Ultimate BASE, and made regular jaunts to the farthest corners of the clubbing map (including a triumphant début at New York's Twilo). Then there's his radio show on Kiss FM, as well as his label and DJ agency. And it was topped off in 1997 when he was named no. 1 DJ in the world in DJ Magazine's reader's poll. Nice one, Mr Nice.

f the now rich history of DJing belongs largely to our cousins across the Atlantic, then in the past ten years, with the arrival of house music to these shores, we have begun to make an impact on the bearing and future of dance music too. One sign of this is the emergence in the early-nineties of UK house's first home-grown DJ superstar: Sasha.

His name (a derivation of his real name, Alexander) has the hint of glamour necessary for a star DJ, containing as it does, the suggestion of eastern promise. Born in Bangor, his early life was a nomadic one, moving here and there until he ended up at a public school in Epsom. "It was the worst move I made in my life. Public school screwed me up completely and I ended up packing my A Levels," he later commented. Returning to his native Bangor, he soon found something to occupy his time. It was 1988 and he discovered the Haçienda. Shortly after, he moved to Manchester and, thanks to a job in telesales, financed the purchase of some decks. His first gigs were just a blag away.

It's only relatively recently that the phenomenon that is Sasha became a truly national one. The buzz was created at a night called Delight at a venue called Shelley's in a place called Longton. Along with Brother in Rhythm Dave Seaman, Sasha created the first truly special post-acid house club. His trademark style was all but patented there. A cappella intros, intense, precise mixing and a wildly varied mixture of records were played. "It wasn't a conscious thing to be different," he said

modestly, "But I just found that I always liked to throw in really mad things."

It was this residency, alongside one at recently-closed Shaboo in Blackpool that created the cult of Sasha. Huge in the north, almost unknown in the south. Inevitably, word began to spread. Bigger and bigger pieces appeared in the specialist press about this talent. Gradually, Sasha moved further south, firstly to Coventry's Eclipse club (then on the crest of the 'rave' wave that had filled the clubs to bursting point) and then to London's Milk Bar. His first cover, with Mixmag, came in December 1991, it posed the question: 'Sasha The First DJ Pin-Up?' Dom Phillips of Mixmag, later interviewed for Altered State magazine claimed, 'People were coming back from Shelley's and saying, 'There are guys queuing to shake Sasha's hand, there are guys asking him to kiss their girlfriends.' It had never been seen before, so we felt we had to write about it."

Sasha had already begun his production career whilst still playing at Shelley's but, during the early-nineties it stepped up a gear as he, by now working with programmer Tom Frederikse, developed his distinctive elongated mixes. "I think DJs who don't want to make their own records are soft, because no-one knows better than a DJ what creates a buzz on a floor."

But the music was changing and Sasha, acutely aware of this, was changing too. Rave had become hardcore; the records were faster and everything was splintering. Time to move on. Geoff Oakes, a keen

clubber at Shelley's was opening a new club in Mansfield. It would be based on residents (Sasha and the then unknown John Digweed) and it would have the attention to detail that Sasha looked for in all his work, whether as a DJ or remixer. If Shelley's and its Manchester forebear the Haçienda had been the innovators, then Renaissance (as the club was to be known) was their distillation. With mock Greco-Roman pillars adorning the club and Mondrian-inspired artwork draped on the stairs, the keyword was style. The queues were soon going round the block. And in a deeply unfashionable pit-town in Nottinghamshire.

After his first, faltering step into production (BM Ex's 'Appolonia') he signed a multi-album deal with DeConstruction, the fruits of which began with 'Higher Ground', an extended piece of modern soul featuring Sam Mollison on vocals. An album, 'Qat', followed, with a surprisingly introspective outlook that eschewed the dynamism of his DJing for easier, more reflective, textures. Since then, Sasha's friendship with Digweed, forged at Renaissance and cemented at joint ventures like their own club Northern Exposure and many double dates behind the decks, has blossomed. Add to that his burgeoning musical relationship with Washington DC-based producer Brian 'BT' Transeau and a residency at New York's Twilo and you have a man considerably more at ease with himself than that embarrassed looking lad who appeared on the cover of Mixmag all those years ago.

"When I first heard house music, I thought my brain was going to explode. I was at the Haçienda and Mike Pickering played 'Love Can't Turn Around' and I thought I was gonna die. The week after, I went back to and he played 'No Way Back' and I just banged my head against the wall and thought, 'fuckin' hell, this is a big orgasm'." A Frenchman in Manchester who fell in love with the music of Chicago and Detroit, and went on to repay the debt of inspiration by merging the sounds he loved into his own broad vision: Laurent Garnier. As well as being France's best-known DJ, the irrepressible Garnier is a crucial junction box in the complex circuits of dance music. He grew up in Paris dreaming of being a professional DJ, wandered through brief careers as hairdresser and then chef (working as a footman in the home of the French ambassador in London and serving the queen, all the royal family, Margaret Thatcher and the French President), and eventually wedged himself into the house scene via a residency at The Haçienda at the height of acid. Starting as a techno purist, making tracks like 'Acid Eiffel', he couldn't contain his excitement for all the different music he loved and was soon known for his rare open-mindedness, driving his long DJing sets with mood manipulation rather than genre isolation. Someone once said he played hardcore you can vogue to, and it's true: he plays techno in all its forms from soulful Detroit to thumping Teutonic, with gay hi-energy disco flourishes thrown in for good measure. He once upset a dance mag by starting his all time top ten with Donna Summer and the Sex Pistols. They wanted a trainspotter's insight into techno. With a neat catering metaphor he confesses, "I haven't found a recipe and I'm not looking for one. I don't want to be pigeonholed into

one style. I'm an open-minded person." He returned to Paris in 1987 determined to put French house on the map. His F Communication imprint did exactly that, as did his involvement with Radio Nova, one of the many independent radio stations permitted by deregulation of the French airwaves in the early eighties. Behind the decks, the voluble, talkative Garnier, a self-declared sex addict, makes DJing a very physical activity. Not for him a static night spent scowling at the levels. "When I DJ, I dance," he says. "I can't understand DJs who don't. How can you give people the power of music if you don't get it yourself? What I play is shakey shakey, wiggle your bottie. It talks to your arse and to your hips. That's the difference between rock and roll and disco."

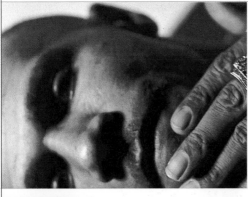

14. Tony DeVit

Brummie Tony DeVit proved that when it comes to dance music, the queens have all the best tunes. His years playing at Trade, sending out pile-driving waves of nu-energy for one of the hardest, most unrelenting dancefloors ever, made him the undisputed ruler of a style of music which post-handbag commercial clubland has now taken fully to heart. He started DJing in 1976, with a long apprenticeship giving gay crowds cheesy tunes from Lipps Inc to Kylie. "I was DJing when it was still a dirty word," he once said.

"Before I collected my wages at the end of the night I used to have to sweep the dancefloor and collect the empty glasses." A 1991 trip to Trade smacked him between the eyes. He gave someone £250 to buy every record he'd heard that night, and that was it. Now his fame is such that Mixmag alleges there's a female clubber in Wales who can't come unless she's shagging to a Tony DeVit tape. Tony died in July 1998, but he won't be forgotten by anyone lucky enough to have heard him play.

15. Grandmaster Flash

In the cut-and-scratch gymnastics of hip hop DJing, Joseph Saddler, aka Grandmaster Flash, stands pre-eminent. He wasn't the first — that honour goes probably to Kool Herc — but he was always the best. In the Bronx warehouse parties of 1976, Herc's system beat him on volume so Flash fought back with technique. A high school electronics student, he was able to rig up a headphone cueing system like he'd seen the disco DJs using. He added the beatbox, an Oberheim DMX drum machine which left the dancers wondering where the record was. His partner's 13-year-old brother invented scratching for him (and became Grand Wizard Theodore) and with his astonishing breakbeat technique, Flash became famous throughout black New York. The rise of the MCs stole the limelight from the DJs, but with the Furious Five behind him, and their sound on chart-bound vinyl as 'The Message', Flash's adventures on the wheels of steel took hip hop downtown and thence to the world.

16. Goldie

Hyperactive future b-boy Goldie was the first to forge true drum and bass stardom, taking breakbeat culture mainstream. An off-the-rails youth who excelled at graffiti and rollerskating (rollerhockey goalkeeper for England), he spent his teens tagging as 'TAT' with a Wolverhampton breakdancing crew, then went to Miami in search of his dad, found gangsters instead and sold gold teeth and airbrush canvases. He returned as rave flowered, and though he kept up with hip hop through his Bristol friends 3D and Nellee Hooper, he fell in love with the breakbeat tunes he heard Fabio and Grooverider playing, appreciating their soul roots. His early tracks 'Terminator' and 'Angel' gave much-needed direction to the fledgling music, and with 'Timeless' and his Metalheadz label he ended the derision jungle had endured and forced its phoenix-like evolution into drum and bass. He even earned enough respect stateside to work with hip hop legends like KRS-1. "If everything falls through, I don't care because I'm an artist who's expanded another avenue," he says. "If I die tomorrow, I don't really care."

17. DJ Pierre

"That old thing?" he laughs. "It's in Chicago, getting fixed. It doesn't even work any more, but I'm going to keep it," a smile, "as a historical object."

The ever-friendly DJ Pierre is joking about a certain Roland 303 drum machine — the one which more than a decade ago created the mutant squelches which were the basis of acid house. He rushes through the well-worn tale in his Southern-inflected Chicago twang: "To make a long story short, my friend Spanky bought a 303. Him and Herb were messing around with it and heard the acid sound. They called me over. I heard it, and I started turning the knobs up and tweaking it, and they were like 'yeah I like it, keep doing what you're doing.' We just did that, made a beat to it, and the rest is history." By discovering the science-fiction noises hidden deep within that particular device, putting them on a record, and calling it 'Acid Trax' by Phuture, Nathaniel Pierre Jones became the godfather of acid house. This new music added rocket fuel to the Chicago fires and started a sound which was to electrify the UK scene and usher in the rave era.

Pierre was one of the energetic young bloods who formed the second wave of house in Chicago, listening from the suburbs as Ralphi Rosario, Farley Keith and the rest of the Hot Mix 5 team were jamming up the airwaves with their ground-breaking WBMX mix show. "Whenever I heard them play two songs at once I wondered how they did it, and that really made me interested in DJing. Then when I graduated from high school, my parents bought me a pair of turntables for my birthday." As 'Nat Jammin' Jones', he contributed to the swell of DJs who roamed the city, playing Italian imports together with the raw Chicago jack tracks, later changing his DJ name to Pierre to escape from the taint of a particular party disaster. When he heard the frenzied funk of DJ Ron Hardy at the Music Box, he was finally alerted to the power of dark underground disco, adding it to his repertoire and going on to build his

reputation playing in parties like Lil' Louis's affairs at the Bismarck Pavilion.

When Chicago's musical explosion died down, he moved to New Jersey, determined to remain part of the industry. Here throughout the nineties, as if having created a whole new genre of dance music wasn't enough for him, Pierre went on to forge another: the slow-building, repetitive, wall-of-sound style which he christened 'Wild Pitch'. Filled with piercing silver strings, dark acidic basslines and complex hard-hitting drums, this was the sound behind such essential Pierre tracks as 'Generate

Power', 'Master Blaster' and a whole artillery of songs with explosion-related titles. Though he is now firmly based in the New York scene, he still proudly declares his love for his hometown. "Everything I make is influenced by Chicago," he says. "That's where I learned to make tracks, so I'm always thinking about Chicago." If you make a visit to the site of the old Music Box, scratched into the black paint of the door frame, alongside numerous tributes to the late Ron Hardy, is a raggedy tag that looks plenty years old. It reads, simply, 'DJ PIERRE.'

18. François Kevorkian

1976, New York, a club called Galaxy 21. Disco legend Walter Gibbons is tearing up the floor with the world's first twelve-inch single, his production of Double Exposure's 'Ten Percent'. A teenage Kenny Carpenter is working the lights, and out in the middle of the dancers, a young French rock drummer is crashing his way through the record's driving rhythms. The club's owner wants the drummer there to spice up the dancefloor, but Gibbons doesn't like it at all. As the night's peak approaches, he tries to throw him off with a rapid-fire sequence of percussion records. He starts cutting between as many drum solos as he can find and a frenzied battle ensues between musician and DJ. Gibbons does his best to trip the drummer up, but the Frenchman, working himself into a flying sweat, matches every track beat for beat. "Unfortunately for Walter, I knew all the solos," laughs François Kevorkian.

Blondie name-checked him together with Grandmaster Flash in 'Rapture', he spun with Larry Levan in the Paradise Garage, he made records with the pioneers of disco, and as he squeezed the stars of the eighties through his dub-drenched disco filter (from Kraftwerk and Depeche Mode to Black Uhuru and U2), he was one of the first people to make a career out of remixing. However, this mischievous dry-humoured Frenchman is no fossil, the tracks he makes today, like 1996's astonishing 'FKEP', and the music he signs to his label Wave, are amongst the most original, experimental, not to say occasionally bizarre, records you could find. He is one of the few DJs whose New York sets attract the new generation of techno-bred clubbers side-by-side with the old-school movers who bring baby powder to sprinkle on the dancefloor. And when he slips back into the classics, you can

believe the Garage never closed. No DJ — no-one — can make disco sound as hard and fresh as François. To put it simply: he's someone who never lost it.

He arrived in New York in 1975 after studying to be a pharmacist. His time as a club drummer was limited, but in constructing demo tapes of his percussion workouts, he realised the amazing possibilities that lay in being able to re-edit tracks. "Being a musician and a drummer, I understood exactly what the DJs were doing, and I also understood what I could be doing that they didn't know."

With his revolutionary home-made re-edits stretching a song's rhythms out to tribalistic lengths, he quickly snared a name for himself as a DJ, and soon fell excitedly into the booming disco industry. When his Galaxy 21 antagonist Walter Gibbons hired him to A&R for Prelude, the single François mixed in his first week (Musique's 'In The Bush') went gold. He soon had Prelude Classics like D-Train's 'You're The One For Me' and 'Beat The Street' behind him, as well as work with Loleatta Holloway and D-Train, and throughout the eighties, did more than anyone to create the modern role of the dance producer, using the developing technology of the recording studio, with techniques adopted from avant-garde electronica and dub reggae, to make dance music the unlimited form it is today. Sitting in the flight-deck of Axis Studios, high above the building that was once Studio 54, François ponders his long career. "A lot of people are one hit wonders, make terrific records and then disappear forever and become taxi drivers. In dance music it's very difficult to last beyond your generation's trend," he says. "I guess I should feel lucky."

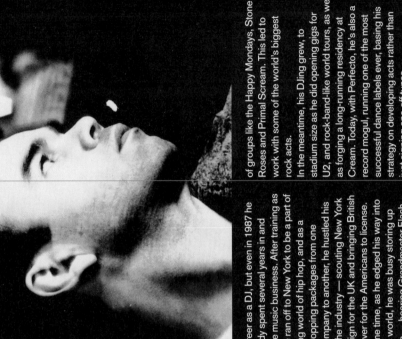

In September 1987, three things arrived on the island of Ibiza: Ecstasy, house music and Paul Oakenfold. A few months later, through strobe-lights and strawberry smoke, while the rest of eighties London was moodily strutting around to rare groove, Oakie was playing the Beatles' 'All You Need Is Love' while his crowd held hands and hugged their way towards the dawn of the acid house revolution.

Paul Oakenfold is a cultural founding father of British dance music, an inescapable angel dropping in on all its most important moments, bringing ideas together and making things happen. Hip hop, acid house, indie dance, mainstream mega-clubbing, Goa trance, stadium DJing, chart records: Oakie done 'em all.

On returning from Ibiza in 1987 he started throwing a Balearic party as an after-hours extension to The Project, a South London soul and hip hop night he was running. He had tried to bring the island's spirit of innocent hedonism to London clubbing before, in 1984, but it wasn't until 1987, with the addition of MDMA, that everything clicked. The Project parties grew into Future, and Future exploded into the legendary Spectrum, a Monday night at Heaven, one of London's largest venues. No-one expected things to happen so quickly. "But I knew something that everyone else didn't," he says. "Which was Ecstasy. We used to go to parties, seven, eight people, and we were all on it. The other 700 people in the club wouldn't know what was happening. So I knew Spectrum was going to go off. I knew it in my heart. That's why I stuck with it."

Acid house provided the launch pad for

Paul's career as a DJ, but even in 1987 he had already spent several years in and around the music business. After training as a chef, he ran off to New York to be a part of the exciting world of hip hop, and as a courier dropping packages from one record company to another, he hustled his way into the industry — scouting New York talent to sign for the UK and bringing British records over for the Americans to license. At the same time, as he edged his way into the music world, he was busy storing up inspiration — hearing Grandmaster Flash and Afrika Bambaataa throwing down breaks or visiting the Paradise Garage and wondering how everyone managed to dance for ten hours at a stretch.

After acid, when the initial UK house explosion mutated into rave, Oakenfold took a different turn, and reinvented himself as a down-tempo remixer and producer, cultivating the dance-inflected rock sound

of groups like the Happy Mondays, Stone Roses and Primal Scream. This led to work with some of the world's biggest rock acts.

In the meantime, his DJing grew, to stadium size as he did opening gigs for U2, and rock-band-like world tours, as well as forging a long-running residency at Cream. Today, with Perfecto, he's also a record mogul, running one of the most successful dance labels ever, basing his strategy on developing acts rather than just signing one-off tunes.

Through all of this, playing records is something he would never be without. "DJing is a ticket to travel the world and I never get bored of travelling. It's an education. DJing is essential to what I do and sometimes you can't get me off the decks. Sometimes you've got to put your feet on the ground and realise you're really lucky, getting paid for this."

22. Tuff Jam

By 1997 the gangsters had maimed jungle and the students had stolen drum and bass, so garage stepped up the pace, snagged back a few demonic basslines, some timestretched vocals, the occasional spinback and gave itself a shot in the arm. Rejuvenated by its new underground status, reclaimed as 'a black thing' and given a name it never really wanted, speed garage was the result — the London sound. Tuff Jam — Matt 'Jam' Lamont and Karl 'Tuff Enuff' Brown were always the leaders of its pack. As DJs, both had soul roots in hardcore clubs and south London all-dayers and they projected themselves into the big time from a residency at The Arches in Southwark, where the Sunday scene, with its Moschino-decked champagne-guzzlers, was born. MCs fought over the right to chat for them, their mixes took the sound chartwards and their prime slot on Kiss FM took speed garage's pirate grooves to the mainstream. "If we don't look after the ship it will sink," they said. "We're trying to keep it cleansed, to keep the goodness in it."

21. Smokin' Jo

London-born Smokin' Jo is one of a growing group of female DJs. Beginning as a model, she worked as an assistant at Gaultier's store in Soho but buying records was her real love. Her big break came when — after playing a few Pussy Posse parties — she was invited to warm up at Trade in Turnmills.

Smokin' Jo's style of music is proof of the misconceptions that surround Trade. Branded as a hard-techno club, Jo's early morning sets started with classic garage, before moving into more dubwise house tracks. Her affection for gay crowds is clear, "If they like something you play, they wave their hands in the air and scream." Her residency at Trade gave her a wider currency as she began to ply her signature sound on the guest circuit, subsequently playing at, amongst others, Pushca, Back 2 Basics and Progress. She now divides her time between the many clubs she plays at and occasional forays into the studio.

20. Danny Rampling

"Acid, acid, acid". Anyone who remembers the early days of Kiss will recall one of Danny Rampling's favourite mantras (usually whispered over some robust 303 workout). It sounds a bit silly today, frankly, but, at the time, it chimed perfectly with what was happening. You could say the same about Rampling himself.

One of the quartet who helped bring the Balearic sound to the UK, Rampling's first night — Shoom — has now passed into club folklore (it would have had to have been held in Wembley Arena if everyone that says they were there really was). After Shoom, Rampling, along with wife Jenni, gave us Pure Sexy then Glam, both mixed-gay parties with door policies as strict as a session with Miss Whiplash.

As dance music went mainstream, Rampling moved from Kiss to Radio One in 1994, where his Lovegroove Dance Party has been a mainstay of Saturday evenings ever since, bringing his inimitable glam techno-hippie persona to a national listenership. His recording, more fitful than his DJing, has produced the minor hit, Millionaire Hippies' 'I Am The Music' on Deconstruction, but it is as a radio host and club jock that Rampling has earned his place at the apex of his profession.

23. Carl Craig

If techno's first-generation trinity of Juan Atkins, Kevin Saunderson and Derrick May were the three musketeers, then Carl Craig would be D'Artagnan, a young outriding blade, the fourth member of a trio. He was still at school when the Detroit scene was at its peak, listening from his bedroom as Derrick May evangelised on the airwaves with his Street Beat radio mix show. He went to the Music Institute, the club which catalysed the city's creativity, he befriended the music's pioneers, he took classes in electronic music and as soon as he could, he showed his genius by making records. As a producer and then as a DJ, Carl emerged as the city's pragmatist, fully capable of working with the restrictive purity of the techno artform, but also a populist fully open to ideas from the wider world of dance music. In doing so, he has been widely praised for breaking the stark fundamentalism of Detroit techno. "I don't want to alienate anybody," he says. "But when I listened to music there were no barriers. No-one said you couldn't listen to Michael Jackson after Kraftwerk."

Carl was an ordinary west Detroit kid and while his techno mentors were turning the sounds of European electronic pop like Kraftwerk, Human League and Depeche Mode into science-fiction soundtracks for post-industrial Detroit, he was most likely to be found in his bedroom strumming on a guitar. The music at home was largely Detroit's earlier creations: Parliament-Funkadelic and Motown, Carl was into 'alternative' groups like The Cure and The Smiths and some of his brother's old acid rock albums by Led Zeppelin and Tangerine Dream, though he was increasingly mesmerised by the futuristic records he heard on Derrick May's radio show.

In 1989 he borrowed a sampler from his college, recorded a set of raw tracks loosely based on elements of May's 'Strings Of Life', tracked the producer down and presented him with a tape. May offered some advice on developing the songs and when Carl came back with the final results, he was so impressed he released them through his Transmat label. One of the tracks, 'Neurotic Behavior', was immediately judged a techno classic, and both the resulting EPs, Carl's debut releases — 'Elements' and 'Crackdown' — remain pivotal reference points for the UK techno scene.

With his deep musicality and a wide range of influences, Carl Craig offers the dance world a stream of important bridges and connections. A track like Paperclip People's 'Throw' brought house and techno forcefully together for a new burst of life, another, 'Bug In the Bassbin' as Innerzone Orchestra wowed the drum and bass community by prefiguring breakbeat jazz. Add to such inspiring syntheses the raw house-techno he makes as 69, or the ambient soundscapes he records under his own name, and you can see why he is treated with such reverence by the anoraked techno cognoscenti.

Although his fame and fortune is in Europe, Carl remains rooted in the Motor City, committed to rebuilding Detroit through its music. "Detroit techno is not new," he says, "but the people in Detroit have not been exposed to it and this shit is a time bomb."

Danny Tenaglia is the latest incarnation of a spirit that has danced joyfully through the New York underground since the days of disco. In a city whose clubland is so steeped in history, this same spirit infuses many of the city's DJs, but no-one can conjure the feelings of the past while playing the music of the present in quite the same way as Danny. Not that he's a preservationist, just that his music shows a deep understanding of the links which tie today's music to the classics of yesterday. As a fellow jock observed, "Even if he plays a record that you don't like, it still makes perfect sense in the story he's telling that night." In short, he is the DJ's DJ, and in a world of egos and bitchiness, it's nice to have his shy, grouchy enthusiasm around. DJing is what I do best," he says, humbly. It's all I've ever done. It's a career, it's my life force." High school held little appeal for Tenaglia and he dropped out, convinced there was nothing there he could learn that would help him chase his dream of being a great DJ. He'd already been spinning throughout his teenage years, but the idea of finishing school to play records professionally didn't exactly fill his folks with pride: "My father nearly killed me," he recalls.

The young Tenaglia spent the next two and a half years playing records at a rollerdisco in his native Brooklyn, a job which coincided with the discovery of a nightclub that was to become his greatest inspiration. The neighbourhood kids would go and brag about the Paradise Garage. I'd be going to other Manhattan clubs like Loft, Inferno, and Starship Discovery. But finally I went to the Garage. And they were right. I was mesmerised. The Garage was it for me from there on."

With compulsive Saturday night attendance here, his Sunday afternoon sessions at the rollerdisco became the place for mad Larry Levan-inspired work-outs, as Danny tried out the songs and techniques he'd heard at the Garage. "It was a big problem because

I was so influenced by Larry, and by the sound that was out there at that time, and by all those records. Sometimes I would leave the Garage and go straight to work, and try to keep that feeling going that I'd been hearing that night. And all these kids trying to rollerskate would bang on the window for me to change the record, they wanted to hear ballads, and Grandmaster Flash and stuff, and I was going off into all this moody funky disco."

After playing in a few Manhattan clubs including Stix and Crisco Disco, a place distinguished by a mammoth can of Crisco on the stage (cooking grease enjoying a certain sexual connotation), he made his mark in Miami in the mid-eighties, with a long residency in Cheers, then the city's

only after-hours club, by importing New York and Chicago house sounds to a lacklustre scene. When he returned to New York five years later, he had made it the busiest dancefloor in the city. Danny's distinctive super-compressed tribal percussion meets the bassline dirtiness of classic dance music to form house that's ever hard and always funky. He calls his music "hard garage", a nod to the club which was his central inspiration, and when a friend heard him spin recently, she declared that she hadn't heard a DJ play like that for years — many years. She hadn't heard a DJ play like that, she recalled, since she heard Larry Levan at the Paradise Garage.

25. Tony Humphries

of the eighties, as disco headed underground and started mutating into house, he yearned for the kind of residency which would let him make his mark. He found the gay/straight melting pot he was looking for in Club Zanzibar in Newark, New Jersey, an intimate club with a superb system, and played there for nearly 12 years. It was here that he helped forge the soulful gospel/R&B-based New Jersey brand of vocal house which (by a slight misnomer courtesy of British journalists) became known as garage, propelling local talent like Freestyle Orchestra, Phase II and Adeva into the big time and putting Zanzibar on the map as one of the world's important places. Through it all he also maintained a constant presence on New York's radio dial, acting as leading tastemaker and breaking literally hundreds of tracks.

When the UK scene started demanding a constant supply of US DJs, Humphries was always top of the list, and in 1993 he even moved over to live in London and played an influential residency at the Ministry of Sound. His music was everything Britain loved about the States: he has always been the quintessential American tune-slinger, a technical master, a phenomenal programmer and that rare contradiction, a stylish purist with an experimental ear. And he says he'll never lose his excitement for playing live. "Once a DJ always a DJ," he says sagely. "Once you've been in front of an audience, and you've been through that excitement of living and dying with whatever happens, then that's always a part of you. After that you always want to play for a crowd, you always have that DJ bug in you."

In New York it goes like this: late one night Tony Humphries plays this incredible song on his WQHT 'Hot 97' mix show. You hum it to puzzled sales clerks at record stores across town. You tape it the following week and play it for them on your Walkman, but end up watching glumly as even the most upfront of them shrug their shoulders and shake their heads. Six months later the track in question is finally released. It becomes, of course, a mammoth club hit. With typical modesty, Tony admits to being just a little ahead of the pack. "I tend to lean on or promote special things a little bit further than maybe other DJs would," he says with a sly hound-dog smile.

Gentle-giant Humphries always makes DJing sound like a serious business. He'll discuss the roots of dance music, how categories and bpms have become so rigid, how different crowds react to different tracks. He'll emphasise the importance of careful programming, the need to avoid

being swept along in your audience's most exuberant moments, he'll stress that you should never forget you're playing other people's songs, and he'll offer careful explanations of what elements he looks for in a record. Above all, Tony will always say that over everything else, his job is to promote new music, he'll always say he's here "to look out for the little guy".

But then, after he's made it sound like a scientific exercise requiring a Harvard degree in mixology, you listen to him play, you close your eyes and let your dancing feet drift onto the floor as beautiful soul-soaked voices weave between lush instrumentation and driving funk-filled basslines. Just by the life he breathes into it and the context he slips it into, Tony Humphries can make an average record sound great and a great record sound truly spiritual.

Born in Brooklyn, he started his career DJing around Manhattan, but by the dawn

26. Judge Jules

Born Julius O'Riordan, Judge Jules acquired his nom-de-Technics while he was studying law at LSE and running clubs at the same time. "When I started DJing it was a wally's job. The qualifications were a football haircut and a loud shirt."

Organising rare groove parties alongside the likes of Norman Jay in the eighties, he discovered house on a trip to New York and began playing it. Gigs at outdoor raves like Sunrise and Biology followed.

A Kiss FM DJ from their pirate days, he remained with them as they became legal in 1990 and presided over their highest rated show until Radio One poached him in the Autumn of 1997. He joined the Manifesto label, a subsidiary of Polygram, in 1994 as A&R where he has scored some notable successes, including Wink's 'Higher State Of Consciousness'. Much maligned as a purveyor of cheese, he has always defended himself vigorously (as one would expect with the name Judge): "I'm the one taking chances. My set might be on 'Now That's What I Call Dance Vol 57' in six months' time, but the fact is you're hearing me now, not then." He remains one of the clubland's most popular and sought-after DJs.

27. Mixmaster Morris

"I think therefore I ambient." Morris is the man who came to the rave but didn't dance — a nutty evangelist for ambient music in all its forms, though he avoids the word 'ambient', as often as possible (he prefers constructions like eg, 'triangle'—TRIp-hop Ambient juNGLE). He got his start working with The Shamen in their early Synergy parties and progressed by a desire to DJ anytime anywhere. In the future he hopes "to have passionate affairs via teledildonics, to ride a big chopper through the metaverse and to make cathedrals in cyberspace." Catch him in a muddy rave tent wearing a silver top-hat and his famous holographic suit, huddled over a spaghettied pile of electronics, producing a soothing waterfall of beatless meanderings. His CD 'Global Chillage' (as Irresistible Force) was one of the prescribed deathbed treatments for ailing acid guru Timothy Leary.

28. Graeme Park

One of the many to enjoy a sustained residency at the Haçienda, Graeme Park first cut his teeth at Nottingham's Garage club in the mid-eighties, playing a selection of funk, electro and early house. Originally from Aberdeen, he met Mike Pickering, then Haçienda resident, at a photo shoot and they immediately hit it off, with Pickering inviting Park to deputise for him shortly after.

It was at the Haç that Park's reputation as a DJ with an ear for classic soulful house was cemented. Before Sasha was ever heard of, Graeme Park was the north-west don, the DJ everyone wanted to emulate and become. He began to move into production in the early-nineties with a string of remixes, including Brand New Heavies' 'Back To Love', but of late appears to have stuttered to a halt. His afternoon show on Kiss 102 in Manchester demonstrated his natural aptitude for radio DJing, with his easy, laconic style winning many admirers. Although his star as a club DJ has diminished, he is still one of the best DJs the UK has produced.

Jazzy M may not be the most obvious name to check, but when the history of British house music comes to be written, his name will be somewhere near the beginning of it. Whilst Graeme Park was pushing house in Nottingham at the Garage and Mike Pickering and Jon Da Silva were doing the same at the Haçienda, Jazzy's work in the south paralleled their efforts. He was the first to host a regular house show on pirate radio. He worked in the first store in London to regularly stock and promote house. And the first release on his label, Oh-Zone, was the now seminal 'Chime' by Orbital.

Born Michael Schiniou in London in 1962, Jazzy M always had a keen ear for dance music and he first got his break at 17 years old whilst working as a doorman. "The DJ was, unfortunately, taken away at Her Majesty's pleasure and so I was thrown in. I suppose I became an instant DJ." From there Jazzy began working at Spin-Offs in the Fulham Palace Road where the influential (but largely unknown) Greg James worked. "He was brought over to his country by the Embassy Club as the first ever mixing DJ. He taught the likes of great dance DJs like Froggy and Les Adams." Whilst at Spin-Offs his big break into radio came via the respected (and predominantly reggae oriented) pirate, LWR. Many of today's current DJs have acknowledged the influence Jazzy's show, the Jackin' Zone, had on them. A teenage Darren Emerson (now of Underworld) wrote letters to Jazzy; Balearic pioneers such as Johnny Walker got into house through the Jackin' Zone. His three-hour Tuesday show (and, later, Thursday too) began in late-1986 and soon became a cult hit amongst the small, but growing, band of house aficionados. "As house music started to come in I introduced it into the show. I mixed it up with stuff like Prince and the Minneapolis sound, Strafe's 'Set It Off' and early garage tracks like Harlequin Fours. As more house kept coming in, it would take up an hour of the show; then it took up two hours until eventually it was the whole show."

His own record store, Vinyl Zone, opened in Fulham around the time of the acid house explosion, and soon became a focal point for this new development. Rave organisations like Biology used Vinyl Zone as an office base and ticket outlet for the huge M25 raves which were exploding as a result of the success of West End nights such as Spectrum and The Trip: "You'd get as many as a thousand people passing through the door on a Saturday to buy tickets," says Jazzy. Through his connection with Balearic DJs such as Nicky Holloway and Walker — who worked at Phonogram — he was approached by an FFRR young-gun named Pete Tong and the 'House Sound Of Chicago' compilation series was born; a key move in spreading the gospel of house nationally. The same label later also gave rise to UK acts such as D Mob, Bang The Party and Richie Rich.

Pete Tong's friendship with Jazzy M also came in handy when he launched both his label, Oh-Zone, and unwittingly, Orbital's career. "It sold ridiculously fast and we didn't really know what to do because we'd never run a label before, so because of my connections with Pete, he came in very strong on it." A few months later 'Chime' was in the national chart and Orbital were the UK rave scene's first pop stars.

Subsequently, Jazzy began to reap the rewards of his groundbreaking work in the eighties, with residencies at Release The Pressure (at the Café de Paris in London)

30. Masters At Work

One is 'Dope', the other is 'Little'. Kenny Gonzales is the big man, born into hip hop, the Borinquen with the Brooklyn beats. Louie Vega is the small guy, the Bronx-bred DJ whose hard, Latin-flavoured club nights bring the NYC house industry together, a tunesmith who inherited the melodies of salsa from his saxophonist father and his singing star uncle. Together, you know them as Masters At Work: phenomenal producers, remixers to the stars, and the track-slinging alchemists behind occasional astonishing four-deck DJ shows. Masters at Work make very special records. Their trademark sound — Latin-spiced tough and dubby house with white-hot percussion, has graced scores of remixes and plenty of huge club tunes — India's 'I Can't Get No Sleep', Lil' Mo Yin Yang's 'Reach', all of Barbara Tucker's anthems, not to mention 'The Bomb! (These Sounds fall Into My Mind)', Kenny's chart hit as The Bucketheads.

And then they bared their Nuyorican Soul. Realising that their records were becoming ever more dependent on live instrumentation, they made a decision to trace the roots of dance, to make songs which took them closer and closer to the

pure Latin music which is in their blood. The result was 1997's ambitious Nuyorican Soul project (A Nuyorican is a New Yorker of Puerto Rican descent), an album which emphasised the continuity between dance music then and now. This studio work brought an older generation of dance musicians together with the current club scene and made for some unique moments. When septuagenarian percussion legend Tito Puente took the stage at Sound Factory Bar with Latin megastar India, then Louie's wife, for India's birthday, the crowd of house-mad regulars went ballistic, a sea of screaming Black and Puerto Rican faces erupting with excitement. Kenny and Louie had to admit that it was a special night indeed. Both had been professional DJs long before meeting each other; Louie spinning in venues across New York: Devil's Nest, Heartthrob and Studio 54; Kenny playing hip hop and freestyle with a mobile disco he called Masters At Work. They joined forces in 1991 courtesy of a mutual friend Todd Terry and a record of Kenny's called 'Salsa House'.

"I thought, with my club music influences, and his hip hop influences together I think

we can make a nice sound," says Louie, recalling the early Masters At Work remixes. "Where it could be hard enough but at that same time have a real soulfulness in the songs and the arrangements." Stacks of records later, the duo continue to make unique, unmissable music, as well as running MAW, their own label and inspiring a whole new generation of producers who work with them in their studio Bass-Hit. Catching their awesome four-deck show is a very rare treat. Though Louie plays nearly every week, Kenny rarely DJs and they have only ever spun together a handful of times. Both, however, agree that DJing is at the root of everything they do. "It triggered everything," insists Kenny. "Everything I've learned is through playing records. Learning the structure of songs, the bars, the breaks, is all through DJing."

"DJing was our training and it still is," agrees Louie, describing how his club nights are the laboratory where work in progress gets tested. "It's so great when we finish something and we get to play it and you see these people like 'Aaaahh!' It's just the playing. I love playing. I love creating with the turntables."

"Shine your light on me Junior!" At the start of this decade, New York's Sound Factory was an unearthly place, the last big truly underground club the city has had, a room where the true believers would leave the world for a few hours and worship the power of dance. For several years it was dangerous, magical, religious.

At the heart of the Factory, ruling over the night like a high-priest, was Junior Vasquez. With epic sets which always lasted at least twelve hours, well into Sunday afternoon, Junior would take his faithful on a magnificent journey, teasing, working, pushing and above all, controlling. He could keep a driving relentless groove going for hours, even while completely changing rhythms, tempos, styles, never once losing your attention. He could work a record for astonishing periods: first tempting you with the tiniest hint deep underneath everything else, then going back to it again and again, exaggerating every great moment until he'd wrung it dry. Few DJs if any have matched the control he wielded over the Factory, and rarely was a club identified with a single person's music as much as here. To the faithful he was a god.

But the Factory closed, New York clubbing started to become lifelessly mainstream, the club's family was displaced by a crowd less pure and Junior vowed never to play anywhere else. For months he kept his word, but in the end, when he realised his beloved club was finally history, he gave up his sacred role and became a mortal DJ. On taking up residence at the Tunnel, he emphasised just what a line he had now drawn under his Factory days. "Everyone has their moment and you can never replace it. I created Sound Factory and in essence and by rights, I should have retired. I should have probably not played ever again. I made my mark."

Donald Mattern, a smalltown butcher's son from rural Pennsylvania, came to New York in 1971 to pursue a career in fashion. His couture career didn't quite take off and he ended up at Downstairs record store, selling tunes to the disco era's greatest DJs. He started DJing himself, began working in the studio with Shep Pettibone and Arthur Baker and, with friends like Keith Haring to help raise investment, started creating clubs. Parties at The Space led to a new club called Bassline which formed the roots of the Factory. At the heart of it was his much-stated desire to recreate the atmosphere of the Paradise Garage. "My Jurassic roots are the Garage," he insists. "That's where I come from. I idolised Larry, and I keep striving, wanting to create that feeling,

that lounge, that booth."

Nowadays, Junior hobnobs with stars from Madonna downwards, remixing whoever he wants and, as dance-ignorant America gets to grips with the troubling idea of the DJ as star, he represents an entire profession for magazines like Rolling Stone. He is famously aloof from the rest of the dance world and less than complimentary about most other DJs. "Everybody else that I had a chance to hear, played the same goddamn way," he'll tell you. "I'd rather have heard myself." And though his maverick attitude and his renowned insecurities have often upset people, his purpose remains clear and sincere: "I never really wanted to be part of the industry. I just wanted to play records and have a party."

32. Harvey

Before the nineties had even begun, Harvey had already been a drummer (he had a single out when he was thirteen), a graffiti 'bomber' and a member of the Tonka Hi-Fi sound system. It was as part of Tonka that he forged his reputation as an eclectic programmer of music, throwing parties in their native Cambridge, as well as in Brighton and London.

Having already been in love with hip hop and electro, he inevitably alighted on house and garage too, and began playing more parties in the London area. Along with partner Heidi, he set up Moist at the Gardening Club and began to bring over some of the greatest New York DJs, including François Kevorkian, Larry Levan and Kenny Carpenter.

After Moist, although he was already running his disco re-edit label Black Cock, it wasn't really until he became a resident at the Ministry of Sound that Harvey came back into the limelight. Playing his fabled mix of disco, house, garage and dancefloor-friendly rock records, his time there culminated in the acclaimed MoS mix-compilation, 'Late-Night Sessions'.

His percussion work has appeared on several records, including the spacey disco-house of Bone's 'Persuasion'. In Summer 1997 he began a monthly residency at the Blue Note in Hoxton, New Hard Left, setting up his own system in the club and playing marathon seven hour sets, the ideal setting in which to see this mercurial eccentric.

33. Jeremy Healy

You could be forgiven for thinking that Jeremy Healy is an awful lot older than he actually is. From his days as a sneering schoolboy punk with lurid green hair, through to sharing squats with Blitz kids like Boy George, Healy appears to have been around forever.

His first brush with fame was with photographer Kate Garner, as one half of the memorably bad dance hoe-down band, Haysi Fantayzee. The group swiftly disbanded after enjoying two hits, 'John Wayne Is Big Leggy' and 'Shiny Shiny' and Healy disappeared from view. He eventually resurfaced in the late-eighties as a DJ (with Norman Jay) at Choice in West London's Subterania. His association with Boy George, established in the late-seventies, continued when the pair collaborated on the E-Zee Posse's 'Everything Starts With An E', a quasi-novelty track that both satirised and captured the spirit of the acid house boom happening at that time. The record, broken by Graeme Park at the Haçienda, eventually became a hit, reaching no. 15 in the charts in 1990.

Healy went on to establish himself as the archetypal superclub DJ with a showy style that included a penchant for Michael Jackson records and Nirvana's 'Smells Like Teen Spirit'.

34. Armand van Helden

A Todd Terry for the new millennium, the New York techno generation's hard house drill sergeant, someone who can wear enough ice hockey gear to clothe the entire Rangers team: Action man Armand van Helden was always loud and vain enough to be on a crash course to stardom. "I don't give a fuck if I'm on the cover of every music magazine. There's no such thing as over-exposure," he blared. He'd like you to think he's an original ghetto-bred Nuyorican b-boy, but he's actually an air-force brat from Boston. His rainbow racial background let him infiltrate every scene Gotham City had to offer, so from raves to Latin block parties, he was there soaking up influences. His records crossed borders, his remixes were central to speed garage's emergence from the underground and his XXL ego might just make him America's first DJ pop star. Desperate to be noticed? He used to walk around the Miami Winter Music Conference with a boombox on his shoulder playing loud jungle.

"Only Coccoluto Plays For Us", read the banner at local football team Napoli's ground one week. That's the kind of devotion that Claudio Coccoluto inspires and not simply amongst his hometown compatriots, but all over Italy, each and every weekend. He's been plying his trade for over a decade now with his distinctive Italian deep sound that is as sensual as it is funky.

Responsible for Naples' Angels of Love club, it is Coccoluto that made it widely recognised as one of the great European discotheques (assisted in no small part by the fanatical Neapolitan hedonists). Under the name Cocodance, he produced single 'Angels Of Love' for NY indie, Maxi Records in 1992, a record which helped give him an international profile.

In 1995, he split acrimoniously with his partners in the club amid much confusion. "We never had problems when the club had financial trouble," he says. "All the problems began when we started to make money," By 1996, with partner Tina Lepre, he established a new club, Arte Dinamica, with a mixture of deep, funky house and theatrical presentations that were both well-rehearsed and visually stunning.

His forays into the studio became more frequent, remixing several tracks for the albums put out by the international DJ organisation, the DMC which are exclusively meant for DJs. Finally he delivered the killer track everyone knew he was capable of: "Belo Horizonti", under the Heartists moniker. Along with studio partner Savino Martinez — the fine resident DJ at Claudio's club — using a sample from Brazilian jazz artist Airto, they created one

of the Summer of 1997's biggest records (and one which has led to a few low-grade, and, in one case, more successful imitations — perhaps predictably). Claudio, along with other Italian front-runners, continues to produce and play his unique deep, meaningful and downright sexy music throughout Europe. As they might say at Napoli's ground, "Coccoluto Only Plays For Us".

36. David Morales

Dance music's largely faceless personae rarely throw up proper old-fashioned celebrities. After all, fiddling about with bits of electronic equipment is hardly likely to attract a Steve McQueen demanding to be shown how an Akai 900 sampler works. But the handsome, chiselled features of David Morales provide one of the exceptions. It's not like he invented house or anything. He wasn't the first DJ on the block either. But as the brief history of dance music unfolds towards the millennium, Morales' name will be the one most likely to be found at the neon-sign manufacturers. Morales, you see, is a bona-fide star. Not like Mariah Carey (who he has worked with), or Michael Jackson (who he has remixed). But in the reduced size universe that is dance music, David Morales is at the summit.

Born in Brooklyn to Puerto Rican parents, Morales was already spinning regularly at his own parties in his early teens and at a club called Ozone Layer. He was also deeply affected by his experiences at David Mancuso's Loft. It was through his DJing in Brooklyn that he came to the attention of New York's leading record pool [needs explaining], For The Record, who recommended him to Larry Levan at the Paradise Garage. "I'd only been to the Garage three or four times. I would spend the whole night staring at the booth and, you know, fantasising, 'I wish it was me up there'," he later commented. As if to confirm the suspicion that Morales' life is charmed, he then got a job at the other hot club in Manhattan, Better Days, where DJ Bruce Forrest was then in residence. His first major Manahattan residency was soon to follow at a new club opened by Maurice Brahms (the man responsible for New York New York in the seventies): the Red Zone. Red Zone was a key club for Morales. It was during this period that he began to immerse himself in the studio where he immediately discovered an aptitude for

remixing, giving birth to a legendary string of mixes, tested at and named after the club. Although remixing was not a new phenomenon, it was house that truly made it an industry staple. And Morales, more than anyone, staked his claim as king of the remixers with a string of reworks that pretty much define the development of house, transforming pop candyfloss like Sheena Easton's '101' into devastating drum-led monsters. Over the following eight years the production line flowed, with each one, somehow, managing to usurp his previous mixes: Brother Beyond, U2, Bjork and D:Ream, as well as producing club classics such as Robert Owens' 'I'll Be Your Friend' and Ten City's 'My Piece Of Heaven'. His work reached its apotheosis with his collaboration with Mariah Carey on her 'Fantasy' album, which was nominated for

a Grammy (the US recording industry equivalent of an Oscar).

His remixing was supplemented by forays into the newly global club culture as its most in-demand DJ. His only break from all of this was to release a flawed album, 'David Morales And The Bad Yard Club', on Mercury in 1993; a confused mix of pop-ragga, house and garage co-produced by reggae master Sly Dunbar. It gave birth to near hit 'In De Ghetto' and not much else.

Today Morales remains a sought-after remixer (although his work has increasingly appealed to commercial DJs rather than his original constituency of underground jocks) and, although he hasn't had a regular residency in New York since Peter Gatien's Club USA closed its doors in 1995, his DJing is still as coveted as his remixing skills.

37. Frankie Knuckles

It's 1981. Frankie Knuckles, a New York DJ relocated for the last four years in Chicago, is driving south through the outskirts of his adopted city to visit his god daughter. He notices a sign in the window of a bar: 'WE PLAY HOUSE MUSIC'. Bemused, he turns to his friend and asks "Now what is that all about?" She looks at the sign and tells him, "It means music like you play at the Warehouse."

It's quite possible that house could have happened without him. Plenty of people claim to have had the same ideas around the same time, and in the same place. However, if you want to say that any one person invented house music, it would be Frankie Knuckles you'd be talking about. Most people would agree that the music takes its name from his club: The Warehouse, an industrial building in west central Chicago. It was here that Knuckles began the experiments that would make him one of the most famous DJs in the world. "By 1981 they had declared that disco was dead," he recalls. "All the record labels were getting rid of their dance departments, and there were no more uptempo dance records. I realised I had to start changing things in order to keep feeding my dancefloor."

By playing re-edited and remixed versions of songs from reel-to-reel, overlaying minimal beat tracks, and even playing drum machines under the mix, Frankie tailored the available music of the time to create the energy he wanted. With a blend of existing disco records and bizarre European imports, all given the added kick of a powerful bass sensibility, house music was born. And a gentle, humble perfectionist named Knuckles became a star.

He had begun by playing in New York in a club called Better Days and, then,

alongside childhood friend Larry Levan, for the hedonistic gay crowds of the Continental Baths (a Bacchanalian entertainment complex of apartments, bars and baths; the same place Bette Midler began her career). When the Continental closed, Levan left to found his own club SoHo (from which The Paradise Garage was to emerge), and Frankie accepted the offer of a residency in Chicago. "I figured what the hell. I gave myself five years. If I couldn't make it in five years then I could always come back home."

Now of course, he is known worldwide for his consummate skills as DJ, remixer and producer. His love for soaring gospel-inspired vocals and heavenly flights of piano has graced scores of dance hits, and lent clubs around the world some of their finest moments. And though today he enjoys an international reputation, playing regularly around the world, Frankie stresses that keeping the energy on the dancefloor takes precedence over the distractions of stardom and celebrity. "I'm there to entertain the audience that's in front of me. And I'm going to give them exactly what they want."

38. Clivilles & Cole

Robert Clivilles (the DJ) and David Cole (the musician) first met at Bruce Forrest's club Better Days where Clivilles was guest DJ and Cole, already a respected session player, was lending a hand on live keyboards. The rapport between the two was immediate, and the first great DJ/musician team of house was born.

The duo wasted no time moving into production and remixing. Their first remix turned Natalie Cole's cover of the Bruce Springsteen song, 'Pink Cadillac' into prime dancefloor food. By 1989, they had already secured their first production deal and had signed to new A&M outlet, Vendetta, where the partnership hit it big with 'Two To Make It Right' and 'Do It Properly' which they did under the pseudonym of Two Puerto Ricans, A Blackman And A Dominican. DJing was equally successful, with Cole accompanying Clivilles' DJing with live keyboards. International recognition came with their next production project: C&C Music Factory and the multi-million selling single 'Gonna Make You Sweat'. The hit factory had finally arrived. Killer remix followed killer production (Lisa Lisa & Cult Jam's 'Let The Beat Hit 'Em', C&C's 'Just A Touch Of Love'), until their profile reached critical mass with 'Pride (A Deeper Love)' which dominated the club charts for much of 1992-93.

Sadly, the work slowed down with only intermittent live appearances from Cole at Louie Vega's sessions at the Sound Factory Bar. David Cole died from an AIDS-related illness in June 1995. Robert Clivilles continues to DJ and produce.

39. Coldcut

This is a journey into sound. As Coldcut, Matt Black and Jonathan More were pioneers of the sampler, sonic mischief-makers among the first to build their records from stolen chunks of other people's. In 1987 'Say Kids What Time Is It?' led the way, but it was 1988's 'Doctorin' The House' and their remix of 'Paid in Full' by Eric B and Rakim that really got the ball rolling. They retreated behind their protégés Yazz ('The Only Way Is Up') and Lisa Stansfield ('People Hold On'), spent a lot of time messing around with computer graphics and multimedia as Hex, and eventually re-emerged as trip hop jazz funkers with their impeccable Ninjatune label. Their milestone club nights like Stealth at The Blue Note were known for mad, bad DJ ideas like having a soundclash with two turntables each, through two sound systems, one at each end of the club. Jonathan More on the Coldcut philosophy — "It's making a joyous sound unto the creator, like a shag on a mountainside with a head full of mushrooms."

40. Deep Dish

Until these Persian princes of melody arrived, Washington DC was known only as the globe's most powerful national capital and for such musical incidentals as go-go and hardcore punk. Then Deep Dish gave the city a dance sound: deep and hypnotic tracks with tricky rhythms and crashing percussion and along with their former collaborators Brian Transeau, Victor Imbres and Jean-Philippe Aviance of Alcatraz, put DC on the house map of the world. Both exiled Iranians, they met in 1992, DJing in the same club. Ali "Dubfire" Shirazinia had survived a period as a trash-can-bashing industrial punk and was playing hip hop, dub and acid jazz. Sharam Tayebi spun a lot of imported house. They busted their DC boredom with investigative trips to New York clubland, hearing Louie Vega and Tony Humphries and meeting Danny Tenaglia. "It felt like the dynamite waiting to explode," recalls Sharam. They returned to sleepy DC and got on with the business of making unique, phenomenal records.

Think of a movement, any movement, and Grooverider has probably been through it. Neither a scene-jumper or scene-stealer, Grooverider has been there from the start. Others may have burned brighter in the dance firmament, but few have stayed the distance.

Born in south London in 1967, drum and bass's principal ambassador earned his tag from his days as a dancer and, somewhat improbably, trained as an accountant for four years before being bitten by the acid house bug.

Originally, a member of the Global Rhythm sound system (playing the classic sound system mix of rare groove and hip hop) Grooverider renounced it all in the name of house, a sound he'd heard through vanguardist Jazzy M. From the first house record he bought — the electronic soul of Mr. Fingers' 'Mysteries of Love' — he was hooked. The remarkable thing about Grooverider is that he has always eschewed the limelight in favour of simply playing what he believed in. Not because of a trend, but because that was what he liked.

"When Fabio and I started playing house and getting called faggots — playing queer boys' music and all that — we just lived with it and took it because we just liked the music," he recalls. "Not because of a vision or anything, but because I just thought it was deeper than anything else that was happening at the time."

With long-time partner and co-conspirator Fabio, he began broadcasting on pirate radio station Phase One, owned by a guy called Mendoza. Through Mendoza they started a club: Mendoza's. Starting in the basement of a house and later in a rehearsal studio in Brixton, it was the crucible in which the laconic pair developed and honed their sound. Kicking-off at 4 am, the tiny club would pick up the stragglers leaving clubs like Shoom and keep them partying through to daylight. It went on for five days a week until the police put a stop to it.

Grooverider's name was really made at the laboratory of breakbeat culture, Rage at Heaven, where from 1990 to 1993 he provided the scene with its first great club. As the house scene was gradually unravelling into disparate factions in the

early part of the nineties, Rage provided a focus for the emerging fusion of hard Belgian techno and breakbeats that gave rise to Grooverider's signature dark sound, with tracks like Beltram's 'Energy Flash' laid alongside the work of Hackney's Shut Up And Dance label.

It was also the club where a young graffitist called Goldie was introduced to this sweaty acid palace. As Grooverider later explained to Muzik, "Goldie had made a tune but didn't think all that much of it. Some geezer gave me a copy of it and I thought it sounded okay, so I whacked it out at Rage. Then this guy with gold teeth comes up to me and says: 'Hey, that's my tune!'"

Subsequent to Rage, drum and bass, so long derided by the music establishment as the bastard offspring of house, bloomed. The previous years in the wilderness explain Grooverider's (and others') jaundiced attitude to the media, but the lack of media interference also provided a springboard for a cohesive movement that rose fully-formed into clubs like Tempo and Metalheadz, a popular Kiss FM show and his label, Prototype, which debuted his own material (under the moniker Codename John). As he states: "It's like the Zulu Nation we're running: You need props, you need unity to make you strong." Via his extensive contacts on the scene, Grooverider helped introduce the dance world to Photek, Dillinja and Ed Rush.

In 1997, the 'Rider released a retrospective compilation, 'The Prototype Years', through Sony subsidiary Higher Ground, affirmation and justification that all along, Grooverider not only did it his way, but that his way was right.

Advice/Support Groups

Lifeline: 101-103 Oldham Street
Manchester M4 1LW. 0161-839 2054
Advice and counselling on all aspects
of drugs.

National Drugs Helpline: 0800 776 600
Open 24 hours for advice on all aspects
of drugs.

Narcotics Anonymous: 0171-730 0009
A 24 hour helpline for people with
addictions.

Samaritans: 0345 909090
Advice and support for any emotional
problems.

Bibliography

The Rise and Fall of the Nine O'Clock
Service
Roland Howard
(Mowbray/Cassell 1996)
An intriguing exploration of the raving
Reverend Chris Brain and his Church of
England cult of God-squad clubbers.

What Kind of House Party Is This
Jonathan Fleming
(MIY Publishing 1995)
A huge collection of interviews and
snapshots from the house decade.
Sprawling, disorganised and hideously
unedited, but occasionally rewarding.

Nightfever. Club Writing in the Face
1980-1997, Richard Benson (Ed.)
(Boxtree/Macmillan 1997)
Like the title says, all the best stuff from
the magazine.

Altered State, The Story of Ecstasy
Matthew Collin
(Serpent's Tail 1997)
Know your history. The definitive account
of how Ecstasy and house music
changed a nation. Unmissable.

Disco
Albert Goldman
(Hawthorn Books Inc. 1978, US Only)
This long out-of-print classic is one of he
most sought after historical accounts of
dance music history. Rightly so too, not
least for its excellent account of the
history of the club DJ.

The Last Party: Studio 54
Disco and the Culture of the Night
Anthony Haden-Guest
(William Morrow 1997, US Only)
Great on the social scene in New York,
very weak on the musical/DJ side.
Occasional sloppy error mars it, too.
Due out in the UK sometime in 1998,
apparently.

Studio 54: The Legend
Domitilla Sartogo (Ed.)
(Neues 1997, US Only. Distributed in UK
by Art Books International)
Mainly pictorial account of Studio 54
heyday, with text by Anthony Haden-Guest.

The Drag Queens of New York
Julian Fleischer
(Riverhead Books 1996, US Only)
Entertaining history of the New York's
drag queen scene.

Downtown
Michael Musto
(Vintage Books 1986, US Only)
Excellent trip through downtown New
York in the mid-eighties with Village

Voice columnist Michael Musto,
including everything from the Mudd Club
to performance artists like Joey Arias.

Take It Like A Man
Boy George with Spencer Bright
(Sidgwick & Jackson 1995)
Riveting and brutally honest saunter
through the life of one of the UK's most
endearing and enduring club characters.

Leigh Bowery: The Life and Times of
an Icon
Sue Tilley
(Hodder and Stoughton 1997)
Affectionate first-hand account of
performance artist Leigh Bowery,
a fixture on the London club circuit from
Taboo to Kinky Gerlinky.

The New Beats, S.H. Fernando Jr.
(Doubleday 1994, US Only)
Exploration of the roots of hip hop culture.

Rap Attack 2: African Rap to Global Hip Hop
David Toop
(1991 Serpents Tail)
Still the best book written on the rise of
hip hop.

Design After Dark:
A History of Dancefloor Style,
Cynthia Rose
(1991 Thames and Hudson)
How club culture influenced graphic
design and vice versa. A visual treat.

Fly: The Art of the Club Flyer,
Nicola Ackland-Snow/Nathan Brett/
Steven Williams
(1996 Thames and Hudson)
The art of the flyer, with a gallery of full-
colour reproductions.

"I wouldn't ever go over there and play Ministry. It's just stupid. Everybody does that."
Junior Vasquez, 1994

DANCE NATION 5
MIXED BY PETE TONG & BOY GEORGE

35 of the hottest tracks and remixes
Plus a 24 page guide to the MOS World Tour

"The only reason that cocaine is such a rage today is that people are too dumb and lazy to get themselves together to roll a joint." Jack Nicholson

The Quiz answers

1 a) Arsenal b) Hartlepool (Apparently, Louie took in a Freight Rover Trophy first round game at Victoria Park a few seasons ago after playing at Shindig in Newcastle. He's been an avid follower of the 'Pool ever since); c) Juventus d) Chelsea .
2 a) Kleavage.
3 c) Overweight Pooch
(and who thought of that name?)
4 b) Francis Nicholls.
5 a) Electribe 101.
6 a) 3; b) 1; c) 4; d) 2.
7 d) the Morales mix of De La Soul's 'Saturdays'.
8 b) Detroit (although we'd rather like to think of it as Barnsley).
9 a) Andy Weatherall
10 d) Vince Montana.
11 b) Vice Cream
12 a) 3; b) 4; c) 2; d) 1.
13 a) Mood Six
14 b) Orbital.
15 c) Goldie.
16 b) Lipps Inc. As Homer says in an episode: "I haven't felt this way about a song since 'Funkytown,'" something we wouldn't disagree with.

Credits

Design by Intro. www.introactive.co.uk

Picture Research by FILMER

Editorial Photography: Ewan Spencer p.2,6,8,14,24,30,32,37,45,62,66,68,72, 74,76,78,80,82,84,90,94,96,126,127

Thanks to: XL Records, RCA Records, Virgin, Ovum Records. FFRR, Fifty First Records,Twisted America, Talkin' Loud. Ninja. Deconstruction, CBS Records – Bill Brewster, Conrad Johnston, Constantine McCrae, DJ Dan, Michelle Allerdyce, Chris Mellor @ DJ, Rachel Leach @ MOS, Flyers – Gavin Fernandez, King St. Records

Visual Contributors:

Jenny Acheson p.109
Jamie B p.99
Guy Baker p.34,41
Devlin @ Plum Source p.118,120
Antony Hague p.111
Ben Jennings p.12,42,61,62,63,64
Mark Mcnulty p.115,42
Mamad Mossedegh p.119
Ministry of Sound Archive p.29,34,36, 100,114,116,121
Daniel Newman p.38,41,42
Redferns p.107
Retna p.16,38,39,60,65,101,103,104, 106,108,112,124
Richard Reyes p.39,43,53,55,59,63,65, 99,101,107,115,119
Rex Features p.70
Science Photo Library p.51
Dave Swindells p.38,39,43,47,49,63,86, 111,115
Telegraph Colour Library p.92
Andrew Testa p.26,41

www.ministryofsound.co.uk

Non-stop clubbing from Ministry of Sound

2 live audio and video broadcasts from Ministry of Sound each week

Over 48 hours of the world's greatest DJ sets

All Ministry of Sound tour dates including Ibiza dates and line-ups

Live video chats and interviews from the likes of Erick Morillo and LTJ Bukem

Ministry Vinyl
The ultimate on-line vinyl shop

Winner of the 1998 Musicweek CAD Award for Best Music Web Site

Weekly E-flyer update of what's happening at the world's most famous club

Clubbers log-on for live chats

The E-Shop
All Ministry of Sound albums and merchandising at low prices and speedy delivery.